What the re
"Keen-sighte
nique of wri

— *The Windsor Star*

"By placing him where he was most comfortable — in the midst of his large and loving family — we are afforded a new insight into the character of the man who knew both uncommon fame and 'terrible despairs'."

— Victoria *Times-Colonist*

"Elizabeth Kimball writes with great wit and charm, recreating the marvellous atmosphere of Leacock-land so that you can practically feel the texture of the rug in her grandmother's parlour, and inhale that giddy compound of whiskey, outdoors, tobacco and tweed..."

— *Wallaceburg News*

Presenting Goodread Biographies

The Goodread Biographies imprint was established in 1983 to reprint the best of Canadian biography, autobiography, diaries, memoirs and letters in paperback format.

Books in the series are chosen from the hardcover lists of all of Canada's many publishing houses. By selecting a wide range of interesting books that have been well received in the bookstores and well reviewed in the press, we aim to give readers inexpensive and easy access to titles they missed in hardcover. A new selection of books is added to our series twice yearly, every spring and fall.

You'll probably find other books in the Goodread Biographies series that you'll enjoy. Check the back pages of this book for details on all titles in the series. You'll find our books on the paperback shelves of your local bookstore. If you have difficulty obtaining any of our titles, get in touch with us and we'll give you the name of a bookstore near you which stocks our complete list.

MY UNCLE, STEPHEN LEACOCK

ELIZABETH KIMBALL

GOODREAD BIOGRAPHIES

Copyright © Elizabeth Kimball, 1970.
All rights reserved.

This book is dedicated to my grandmother, Agnes Butler Leacock.

Quotations on pages 2, 48, 107, 115, 119, 121, 129, 133, 134 from the book, *The Boy I Left Behind Me* by Stephen Leacock. Copyright © 1946 by May Shaw. Reprinted by permission of Doubleday & Company, Inc.

CANADIAN CATALOGUING IN PUBLICATION DATA

Kimball, Elizabeth.
    My uncle, Stephen Leacock

Originally published under title: The man in the Panama hat. Toronto: McClelland and Stewart, 1970.

ISBN 0-88780-124-2

1. Leacock, Stephen, 1869-1944 — Biography.
2. Authors, Canadian (English) — 20th century — Biography.*
3. Humorists, Canadian — Biography.   I. Title.
II. Title: The man in the Panama hat.

PS8523.E22Z71 1983   C818'.5209   C83-099193-X
PR9199.2.L42Z71 1983

Published in 1970 by McClelland and Stewart Limited
First published in paperback 1983 by Goodread Biographies
Canadian Lives series publisher: James Lorimer

Goodread Biographies is the paperback imprint of
Formac Publishing Company Limited
333 - 1657 Barrington Street
Halifax, Nova Scotia
B3J 2A1

Printed and bound in Canada

Dedicated to my grandmother, Agnes Butler Leacock

	Introduction
1	Leacock Land 1
2	... and its People 16
3	My "not most remarkable" Uncle 26
4	Early Intimations 33
5	Legend Becomes Flesh 45
6	The Corkscrew Sequence 52
7	The House at Old Brewery Bay 56
8	The Birthday Party in the Bush 67
9	Pater Familias 76
10	... and Genial Host 88
11	An Expedition to the Farm 100
12	Frost Flowers in the Night 112
13	... and Sunlight Through the Clouds 119
14	The Boy He Could Not Leave Behind Him Part I – England 128 Part II – Canada 138
15	You, too, Can Bake a Cake Like Stephen Leacock's Mother Used to Make 149
16	A Funeral at the Lake 159

Thank You, Thank You, Thank You...

Will the following please step forward and receive my grateful thanks?

Helen Phelan, for putting into my head the idea of writing this book;

and *Paul,* her husband, for providing the boat upon which this notion was proposed; and for his personal recollection of my uncle, which opened the gate to Memory Lane.

Dick Burrowes, my brother, for digging out of his attic the tattered bits and pieces of paper which became research material;

Stephen and Margaret Burrowes, my brother and sister, who acted as patient consultants on our common past.

Stephen Leacock, my cousin, for his encouragement and approval of his project; for his generous sharing with me of his personal memories of his father; and for the benefit of his judgment on several artistic problems I encountered in writing *The Man in the Panama Hat.*

and to all my other cousins, family connections and friends who accompanied me down Memory Lane in search of clues. And especially Tina; to talk to her was like visiting Old Brewery Bay when my uncle was still alive.

A very special Thank You to R. B. Pattison for the inspiration that his paper, "Stephen Leacock at Play" afforded me, and for his permission to quote from it.

Thank you, too, dear, gracious inhabitants of the English provinces of Leacock Land...

Mr. and Mrs. Vincent Green, whose unstinting hospitality I enjoyed at Leacock House, in Swanmore, Hants.

Hew Butler, my cousin, his wife Joanna, and the incomparable Hannah, their daughter, for making me feel so much at home in Bury Lodge.

Mr. and Mrs. Wilfrid Haig Loyd, for their hospitality at Oak Hill, Isle of Wight.

Peter ffrench-Hodges, and staff of British Travel Association, for aid in discovering my family's bit of England;

and to other people and organizations too numerous to mention who assisted in the task.

Introduction

The Man in the Panama Hat is Stephen Leacock . . . my Uncle Stephen, my mother's older brother.

I rarely saw him in winter, and never in the famous coonskin coat, which was, according to legend, an ancient, scurvy garment, held together with safety pins.

It was almost always summer when I saw him, at my grandmother's place in Sutton, and he generally wore a Panama hat. But I believe all the stories about the coonskin coat, because the Panama was battered and yellowish, and looked as if it had been born old.

This is not an ambitious book . . . not a biography, filled with facts and figures – not an analysis of his character or his work. I have neither the aptitude, nor the inclination, for such scholarly works. Dates confuse me, what the world calls facts bore me. And I don't like backward looks.

Yet I knew him little, and more closely, in a different way, than most of his biographers. He visited at my grandmother's; my brothers and sister and I visited him. And my mother and my aunts and uncles talked a lot about him. The little I experienced personally, plus everything I heard from my elders, and the considerable amount I absorbed through osmosis, gave me a knowledge of him that a world which is mainly made up of people born when he was old, or after he was dead, cannot have. To them, my little knowledge may seem much.

These are my recollections, my impressions, and a few interpretations of my uncle. They will include a bit about the part of earth which he inhabited – the England of his early boyhood; the farm at Egypt; Sutton; Orillia. For not only is no man an island, but the lands he loves, and in which he lives, shape him, and tell us of him as surely as the clothes he wears.

I will tell you, too, about his family; a little about his wife and son, a great deal about his mother, his brothers and sisters . . . not only because they were part of his scene, but because Stephen Leacock was very much a family man.

In the chapter on the family I will give the grown-ups, at least, their proper names; after that they will be simply "Teddy" and "Dick," "Dot" and "Missie," just as they were to my uncle.

You will find few of the stories about Stephen Leacock with which you may already be familiar; and that is deliberate. They are good stories, most of them, but you already know them. Sadly, you will not find very many "funny stories" you *haven't* heard. Partly because, it seems to me, all sources have been milked dry long ago; and partly because, as my Aunt Mary remarked, so much of the Leacock humour depended upon the momentary situation and the intonation of the voice; even Stephen Leacock's jokes, some of them, would suffer in translation.

So now let me invite you to look, as it were, through a hole in the hedge, at Stephen Leacock with his family . . . his mother, his brothers and sisters, his nieces and nephews, his wife and son, the people who worked for him. Seeing him thus, and with eyes not wholly awed, it is hoped you may come to know my uncle as a person rather than a personage.

Let me help you part the branches. Come, let's watch the man in the Panama hat.

1

Leacock Land...

Our common terrain... Uncle Stephen's and ours... was Granny's Lake. He was on one side and we were on the other; he visited us and we went over to his house, singly or in sets. And although each one of us had a personal map which included places of no importance, or were unknown to other members of the family, Granny's Lake was on every Leacock map.

As far back as I can remember, summer was Granny's Lake. Literally, my memory begins the summer I was three, and had my arm in a sling because I had broken it. I fell down in the lake and got the sling wet, and one of my grown-up Sheppard cousins scooped me up to safety. There memory begins, with the comforting face above me, framed in the leaves of the big willow tree at Sibbald's Point.

If you cannot find Granny's Lake on ordinary maps, do not try. Later, much later, I discovered that, strictly speaking, it was not Granny's lake at all; that people outside the family called it Lake Simcoe. However, although these unfortunates have the law on their side, I do not think there can be any reasonable doubt that my Granny was the heart and core of this wonderful body of water, and Granny's cottage was its headquarters. Granny's Lake was the only lake in the world. Or so I thought when I was a child. Eventually, when I found that there were other bodies of water, which not only claimed to be lakes, but had their claims honoured by my school geography, I continued to feel that it, at any rate, was the only lake that mattered. I still do. It was the biggest, the bluest, the most beautifully bottomed. (Stripey yellow sandbars, soft as my mother's Turkish carpet beneath our feet, at Granny's cottage; green and pink and blue and yellow stones at Sibbald's, cruel to the feet but satisfying to the eye and soul.)

All the uncles and aunts, all the cousins, and all our friends, felt the same way about the Lake. In *The Boy I Left Behind Me* Uncle Stephen only put into words what we all felt: "Here the blue of the deeper waters rivals that of the Aegean; the sunlight flashes back in lighter colour from the sand bar on the shoals; the passing clouds of summer throw moving shadows as over a ripening field, and the mimic gales that play over the surface send curling caps of foam as white as ever broke under the bow of the Aegean galley."

His first glance, when he arrived at Granny's cottage, was always for the lake. Innocent alike of the existence of the Aegean, and of my uncle's familiarity with that sea, we could not know that he was checking out her charms against those of our lake, like a man in love who cannot ever quite believe his good fortune.

I know what must have been in his heart in these moments. I have only to go back in memory to the moment when, on our way up to Granny's at the beginning of each summer, we got our first glimpse of the water and now, as then, my heart feels full enough to burst. The beauty of the lake came upon us head on, and engulfed us utterly as true love must. There it was . . . our Granny's Lake . . . blue and smooth and still as the sky above, or dancing with waves and scintillating like a twenty-fourth of May sparkler. It was always hard to believe it was still there, after the long winter of exile. Still there, and filled with promise of days that would scorn the clock with their volumes of delight.

The geography of Granny's Lake is simple. Imagine yourself standing with your back to Toronto (the only sensible thing to do in summer). You are now facing Granny's Lake, which is about fifty-two miles from Toronto. Granny's cottage and the rest of her territories are right at the bottom of the lake. At the top, at Orillia, is Uncle Stephen's house. The only other places of any importance are (on Granny's side) the Farm at Egypt, and Uncle George's house, "Meadowlea," at Aurora; and Beaverton (on the way to

Orillia), where Granny lived with her younger daughters when Uncle Stephen was young, and where Aunt Carrie lived when I was a teenager.

On Granny's side of the lake were also her house at Sutton West, which was connected to the cottage by the Black River; and several other dependencies about which I will tell you shortly.

Even if you do not believe that Granny's Lake is the *only* lake in the world, you still cannot mistake it, for it is certainly the largest, bluest, and most beautiful. It has a more brilliant sparkle, bigger waves, and whiter white-caps than any other body of water with the possible exception of some as yet undiscovered ocean. It is older than time and younger than four o'clock in the morning. It needs no Circe to sing; the voice of its waves, on a bright morning, would woo the most strongly confirmed land-lubber to at least its shores. And on a day when skies are black, and the waves roar and crash on the rocks at the foot of Granny's cliff, Circe would sound as thin and silly as a chorus girl competing with Chaliapin.

You cannot hear the lake, of course, till you are near its shores, even on a windy day. But not long after you leave the little town of Sharon Hill behind you, you will see it from the brow of the hill, as you drive to Jackson's Point. And whether it is a calm day, and the lake the pale, lustrous blue of the ribbons on an infant's bonnet; or whether, on a day of brilliant sunlight, it flashes like a basketful of diamonds thrown upon a sapphire slab; or whether it is a day of cloud, and it shimmers like the deep blue satin of the Queen's Order of the Garter you will see at once that everything I have said is true.

Once you have first sighted the lake, I do not need to urge you to hurry. Coast down that hill, lickety split, and do not slow your car till you come to Jackson's Point. Then point east or right, and drive about a mile and you will come upon my granny's cottage, perched right at the top of a golden sand cliff, on the lake side, and hidden by a high cedar hedge.

(To do this, you must literally retreat temporarily some thirty years, for Granny's cottage no longer stands where it did while she was alive. It has been moved across the road and a little bit east, and is now, I understand, used as a guest cottage at the Briars Golf Club, across the road.)

When I was a child, Granny lived in the house at Sutton, about four miles distant. Visiting sons and daughters who had children usually stayed at the cottage. We did not often stay overnight at the house in Sutton, although often we went up to see Granny, and she came down to the cottage almost every afternoon. Not to see us, I later realized, but to see the lake. I will tell you more about the house later. Granny's cottage was not, literally speaking, Granny's at all, for she leased it from Jack Sibbald of the Briars. I have heard that it was the first summer cottage built between Jackson's Point and Mossington's. When I first remember it, there were still large vacant fields between the few cottages along the lake side of the shore. I recall Jack Sibbald sometimes dropping in to talk with Granny, an event which I am sure was purely social, but Uncle George insisted that there was an ulterior motive in Mr. Sibbald's concern over my grandmother's health, since, having originally stipulated, back in about 1918 or 1920, some such modest rent as $50.00 for the summer, delicacy forbade his raising the rent. Nor, as would have been even more profitable, did he feel he could raze the cottage, which stood upon two hundred feet of pure-gold lakefront, and build and rent a larger, more modern house. As Granny lived to be ninety, the business man in Jack Sibbald must often have winced at the high cost of friendship. After she died, he moved the cottage to the Briars Golf Club and the two lots upon which it had stood were sold or leased.

However, in all but title, it was most certainly Granny's cottage. Filled with her furniture and her descendants, shaped to her way of life, it was as distinctively Agnes Emma Leacock as the knobbly white canvas "sneakers" and the floppy white cotton cap ("Mother's cricket cap," Uncle Stephen called it) which she wore when she came to it.

It was a long, one-storey bungalow, with most of the rooms opening on a low narrow verandah facing the lake. My mother had told us that this was the style of houses in India, and this, in my eyes, gave the place an especial exoticism, as did the acacia trees amongst which we played house, ("Grown from seeds Old Captain Sibbald brought back from India," our mother claimed).

At any rate it had, as I recall, three bedrooms to one side of the living room, the smallest being next the kitchen and used for the little maid from Sutton whom Granny supplied with the cottage, and the largest reserved for Granny when she stayed there. At the opposite end, farthest from the kitchen, was a bedroom which was particularly popular with the children, since not only could one eavesdrop on the adults' conversations in the adjoining sitting room, but one could hear, through the thin wooden wall, the approach of visitors along the path from the gate. One could also hear the cars as they sped along the hedge-lined road.

The living room, however, was the wonderful room. It was panelled entirely with horizontal slabs of cedar-wood which still had the rough bark on them and, by way of hiding the joins, I suppose, and for decoration, grape vine wound its way around the doorways and window frame. There was a fat little stove near one end, around which, on cool evenings, my mother and Aunt Carrie and their visitors would gather, chattering and, annoyingly, whispering when they got to some really interesting bit of gossip, and drinking endless cups of tea. This room had also what surely must have been the first picture window in any Ontario, if not in any Canadian, summer place. It is true it was not one large pane, but many small square panes, but it covered one wall almost entirely. Beneath it was a lumpy old couch, from which it was my special delight, during storms, to watch the lightning forking down into the turmoil of waves, and the thick Oxford-grey clouds massing and moving across the obscured sky.

The verandah ran along the lake side, and, as far as we children were concerned, could not possibly have been anywhere else, since if we were not *in* the lake, we must at least be within sight of it. (It was on this verandah that Uncle Stephen threw the corkscrew at me. I'll tell you about that later.) The grown-ups ate at one end of the verandah; and when we were little we ate at an oilcloth-covered table on a little verandah one or two shallow steps below the verandah proper. The kitchen lead off this tacked-on verandah, and everyone had to traffick through it to get to the "closet" at the back. (We had never heard the term "privy" except in connection with the Privy Seal in England, and I still cannot refer to the place where I keep my clothes without thinking of the neat little house, whitewashed within, painted brown outside, and embowered in cedar trees, whose aromatic scent mingled with the clean astringent odour of chloride of lime.) The closet accommodated two, but since the morning visit was social as well as therapeutic, there was considerable milling about on the kitchen verandah, as an impatient queue waited for seats. You weren't allowed to go out in Uncle Charlie's boat, or down to Mossington's, or bathing until you had been to the closet.

There were chamberpots in the bedrooms, but they were very rarely used, since, hardly little Britishers-by-remove that we were, we would have been scorned as "soft" had we resorted to them, even on the coldest, wettest night. This fact was imprinted upon my memory by the terrible screams, one night, of the little maid who, shirking the trip to the closet, had cut her bottom on the broken lip of a chamberpot. Although the wretched girl had to have several stitches in her buttock, my mother's compassion was tempered by scorn of the girl's self-indulgence.

There were washstands, too. Actually, they were curtained-off corner shelves, upon whose top sat the basin and pitcher and soap dish, with its fat bar of marbled, lividly pink or green soap. The chamberpot was hidden beneath a cretonne curtain. There was no running water in the cottage, for which fact we were grateful, as a part of our morning duties was filling the wash-pitchers from the pump. Not only did we, of course, enjoy this excuse to play with water, but the pump stood on the edge of an excitingly steep bank. Normally, the cliff-brow was forbidden, but the ban was overlooked in this instance for practicality's sake. From the edge of the cliff we could see the thin galvanized pipe leading from below the pump to, as it seemed to us, miles out in the transparent water. Yes, we drank it; Lake Simcoe, now declared polluted, was that clean all those years ago.

At the end of the verandah opposite the kitchen and the pump and the closest was an expanse of grass and sand grandly called "the lawn." The grass was very fine and soft, like a dryad's hair, but although it was very long, it never needed cutting because there was such a steady traffic over it that it never got a chance to stand up straight. Also, at "the children's end" (the end near the verandah was reserved for adults) it had big bald spots, where little girls had traced hop-scotches, or where generations of Red Rovers had "come over," but not without digging in their sandalled, sneakered toes with all their might before the final, turf-destroying yank.

The whole lawn was meant to be reserved for adults, the acacia groves being the children's territory; but we were allowed to play at the west end for birthday parties (which occurred at least once a week, it seems to me – if not for one of the eight summer-resident young, for a visiting cousin from Calgary or Toronto). We were also permitted the west end in the evening – if we were quiet.

Across this end, during the day, the longer grass and the skimpy little bushes were frequently agitated as adventurers of both sexes wriggled their way to the cliff's edge, there to drop down over the brow to its soft golden face. This was forbidden territory; the cliff must have been about thirty or forty feet high, and it was of very soft sand. Small stands of Indian pipes, and tufts of purple-blossomed vetch provided the only hold by which a child, once he started to slide, could arrest his descent to the rocks and water below. But the greater peril – and, I now see, a very real one – was of cave-ins. For, emulating the swallows who darted, twittering, in and out of a vast honeycomb of high-rise apartments, we made ourselves caves, digging out the sand with hands and sand-shovels.

Here our whole company played at pirates and smugglers; or, alone, one nursed a hide smarting from the corrective hairbrush-back, or feelings as acutely injured by an adult's scolding, or the teasing of one of one's peers.

At the back of the cottage was Uncle Charlie's Dog House, which was the first I can remember of the excuse houses, which so many of the men of my family erected for themselves as a retreat from the rigours of family life. Uncle Charlie's Dog House was built, I am told, for Airedale, Granny's large, ill-tempered canine who knew no other name but that of his breed. I do not believe that my dear Uncle Charlie could have been so perfidious as to deliberately enlarge the original plans of Airedale's kennel so that it came out to be a very comfy little bungalow for himself, but not only did Uncle Charlie occupy it from the first, but Airedale didn't, except on rare occasions when he was locked up there to keep him from following us on one of our excursions.

The Dog House held, among other furnishings, stacks and stacks of old *Daily Mirrors, Illustrated London News* and *Punch*, so that I was almost prepared to welcome a rainy day. For on rainy days we were sent to play in Uncle Charlie's Dog House and, as the rain eased off, in the narrow lane behind it. Though a long way from being the glorious playground offered by the lake, or by perilous sand caves, or even the acacia groves and the stretches of delicate long grass of Granny's lawn, still the Dog House territory was not a bad place of exile on dull days. The ground was soft yellow sand, shaded by large pines, and by the tall dark cedar hedge which ran almost without any break, except for the gateways of cottages, from Jackson's Point to Mossington's. The pines dropped cones and sprays of needles for the girls to play with, chipmunks and yellow squirrels romped up and down the big trunks, and small birds darted in and out of the hedge. Occasionally, a horse and rider trotted along this narrow passageway behind the cottages, preferring its peaceful shade to the noisy, traffic-ridden road beyond.

A little earlier I hinted that Granny had several dependencies to her cottage. There were three. A little to the west of her, and before you arrived at her cottage, was Jack Sibbald's home, The Briars, a large old red brick house across the road from the lake where we used to get our milk, and, as a major event of the summer, attend the Church Garden Party. The Hall, whose name I later discovered to be Eildon Hall, was where old Uncle Martyn, Aunt Pol, Aunt Addie, Aunt Queenie, Willie Sibbald and a whole lot of little Sibbald descendants lived. Sibbald's Church was to the east, and just before you went through the big gates and down the long drive to Eildon Hall.

Now, since any Sibbald descendant who reads this must be in a towering rage by now, and must be saying "Dependencies indeed!" let me hasten to point out that I only *thought* that Granny owned the Briars and the Hall and the Church. (I knew she didn't own Mossington's Boathouse, but that was only because by the time I was old enough to "hang around" Mossington's, as my brothers and boy cousins rakishly termed this delicious activity, I was also old enough to know better.) But during earlier years I honestly believed she owned everything, including the whole lake.

In reality, of course, all Granny actually owned was her house at Sutton. Far from being a dependency of Granny's, the Hall was the original manor house of an estate of nearly six hundred acres, which is now York County Park. At one time, Granny rented The Grange, a lovely old white stucco house on the estate; my brother Stephen was born there. "Granny's Church" was really Sibbald's Church, and is generally so called, although its real name is the Church of St. George the Martyr. The Briars belonged to Jack Sibbald, a cousin of Uncle Martyn, who was family head at the Hall. All that the rest of us Leacocks owned was six feet each of soil in the Sibbald's churchyard: and sometimes not even that, as we often doubled up cosily in one grave. For example, Aunt Maymee and her husband share a grave, the compact little box containing Uncle Henry's ashes having been let down into a hole just above Aunt Maymee's stomach.

Granny's house was at Sutton, about four miles from the cottage and Jackson's Point. It stood on a big, pie-shaped piece of ground, with its front door pointing toward the Black River, and, across the river, at Laviolette's Ice Cream Parlour. The bank was thickly wooded, and Uncle Charlie had built rustic steps down it, shallow enough for Granny to manage, so that he could take her paddling up the river in her green canoe.

Aunt Dot had built this house for my grandmother. It was grey-white stucco, with three bedrooms upstairs for visiting family, and Granny's and the housekeeper, Lang's, bedrooms downstairs. Granny named it "Bury Lodge" after her uncle's home in Hampshire England, where she had spent most of her girlhood years. It was a funny, cramped house for all its size. ("You will never be able to get my coffin out the door," was Granny's first remark, when she saw its narrow hall; and, truly, she did have to go out the window of her bedroom.)

Into Bury Lodge were crammed all the left-over bits and pieces of Granny's furniture . . . the walnut dining table and sideboard; the little upright piano upon which she used to play us hymns, or, more often tinkle out "A Frog he would a-Wooing Go!" or "The Fox looked Out One Moonlight Night"; the pretty rosewood music rack; the secretary, filled with her diaries from the time she had been a girl; built-in shelves crammed with books beside the fireplace; and underneath them stacks and stacks of *London Mirrors, Sketches* and *Punches* . . . enough to keep a young bookworm in headaches for a whole summer of rainy afternoons.

There was a cushion embroidered with the names of battles of the Crimean War in which Granny's brothers or cousins had fought; mementoes of the Indian Mutiny, brought back by her brother; a sandalwood box carved with tiny mandarins and exotic birds peeping out through branches of flowering trees, which had been filched during the Boxer Rebellion; a minute, twisted lead soldier whom one of the grandsons had swallowed and later been induced to surrender by I know not what agent nor through what exit.

In Gran's bedroom was a frail little desk. ("Mother's folding desk," according to *my* mother, but I doubt if it had folded since the day when Granny brought it back from Natal, in South Africa, where she and Grandfather spent the first year of their married life.) The desk, which now belongs to one of my nieces, was rosewood, and sometimes, as a treat, Granny used to show us the mementoes of her early days which she had kept all these years . . . the hoof of her pet fawn at Bury Lodge; her raven's skull; pressed flowers she had picked from Napoleon's grave on Elba when the ship put in there on their way to Africa; and (I still have this treasure) a wooden doll so tiny it fitted into a child's ring-box. (Less than an inch tall, she has jointed arms and legs, and still wears the little lace pantalettes and ribbon-trimmed dress Granny's mother made for her in about 1846.)

As I have remarked, Bury Lodge always seemed small and cramped, it has since occurred to me that perhaps this was because there were always so many people in it. Granny, Lang and Uncle Charlie were the only actual residents, because the theory was that the house was a quiet haven for Granny after all the tumultuous years she had suffered. But there were always people coming and going, throngs of them, so that if at any one time you had counted heads you would surely have toted at least seven. Uncle George, clattering in with a party of Hunt-Clubbers, in red coats, top hats and heavy boots, here for luncheon or supper before they went on to the Sutton Horse Show. (Uncle George always brought wine and a cold steak-and-kidney-pie from Cole's and, I am sure, he felt that made the entertaining trouble-free for Granny.) Uncle Teddy and Aunt Gypsy and the children arriving from Calgary, and brothers and sisters rushing down from Toronto to see them. Uncle Charlie bringing in a brace of little boys and girls from the village, on their way to Mossington's to fish. Uncle Jim, whom no one had seen for years, appearing at breakfast. ("But the doors were all locked. How did you get in, Jim?" asked Granny. "Through the upstairs window," Jim replied. "Lang," Granny asked her housekeeper, "didn't you hear Mr. Jim coming in?" "Oh, sure, I heard him, Mrs. Leacock, but I said to myself, 'That'll just be one of Mrs. Leacock's boys,' so I went back to sleep.") Uncle Stephen driving up on the "circular drive," gravel flying, the screen door banging, Uncle Stephen called "Mother, Mother, where are you?" before the car door was shut. Daughters and sons filling every bed upstairs, grandchildren stowed away on cot beds, in the covetted "cubby-hole" under the stairs (very popular with eavesdroppers), and in tents behind the raspberry patch. Rag-time and hymns alternating on the wheezy little piano. ("It has a nice tone," Granny would remark, demonstrating the typical Leacock talent for glorification.) Grown-up daughters quarrelling as if they were still in the nursery. ("Girls! Girls!" Granny would chide. "Stop it! You are vexing me.") Uncles roaring with laughter one minute, with rage the next. ("Stephen! Charlie! mind your temper," the tiny white-haired woman would reprimand them sternly.)

Cries of welcome, voices uplifted in farewell. Babies crying, babies cooing. Soft-voiced Indians wishing Granny a good-day; Old Lang's slow voice trying to get a head-count for the next meal. ("Charlie, pick some lettuces and raspberries. Daisy is here with the children.") Earnest conversation and gentle laughter beneath the walnut trees as Granny and the Vicar discussed Scripture over a glass of dandelion wine – her own brew, and filled with an earthy fire more potent, surely, than anything from the Leacock vineyards in Madeira.

Each day began with Granny's six-o'clock cup of tea and her private prayers. She breakfasted in her own room, we in the dining room. Then, immediately after breakfast, family prayers in the living room. Back then to her room with Lang, to discuss the day's menu and compile the grocery list. Then it was the grandchildren's turn to visit, and to receive our daily ice-cream nickel, which parchment-skinned old fingers dug out from a little crocheted miser's purse. After this, "Fetch me my canes," Granny would say. (She had had several toes lopped off in what has since seemed to me a remarkably slip-shod attempt to correct her bunions. As a result of this bit of surgery she always needed two canes.) Then Granny and her *entourage* – grandchildren, perhaps a daughter, and Airedale, or his successor Jake, set out for the village across the bridge. First stop was Laviolette's to get our ice-cream cones, then Burrows Grocery and on to Pugsley the butcher.

Here Granny bore down on the really important business of the day – selecting the "joint" for her table. This transaction was conducted with all the formality of a presentation at the Court of St. James. Pugsley inquired at length, and point by point after Granny's health (or should I say "joint by joint," since her rheumatism was a continuing source of discussion?). Then Granny inquired after Pugsley's health, briefly (the portly gentleman was obviously Grade-A Government approved), and, at length, about that of his family. They discussed my absent uncles' healths, and that of their wives and children. They touched on such local events as St. James Sunday School Picnic, and a threatened change of hours of the Toronto-Sutton trolley. These courtesies attended to, they bore down upon the selection of a "joint" or "rack" worthy of the table at Bury Lodge – although even this matter was led up to delicately, being preceded by a discussion of the merits of meats consumed in the past by Granny's household. Pugsley allowed a demerit here, Granny magnanimously praised a particularly noble roast. Having thus established that Pugsley was, all in all, worthy of his high position as provisioner to my grandmother's table, and that she, on the other hand, was not easily fooled, the lamb or beef or ham was brought down from its hook, reverently laid out on the big wooden block and Pugsley, with the dexterity and dedication of a surgeon, swiftly severed, lanced and sewed the chosen joint. He was then paid off; the dog, whose drool had dampened the sawdust close to the block, was given a juicy bone; farewells were made; and out through the sawdust we scuffed, a favoured child carrying the string bag now heavy with the roast.

Returning home, parties set out for the cottage – children and dog going ahead via the trolley, with, perhaps, the cottage maid (or "the Little Girl," as Granny called her); while Mother, or an aunt, perhaps, might stay with Granny till afternoon, when Jim Bovair of Bovair's Livery and his horse, or (in later years) Oswald King in his taxi-cab, would take them to the lake.

As to the farm, where Uncle Stephen and his brothers and sisters spent most of their childhood, it was on Granny's side of the lake, too, but four miles back from it, at a tiny hamlet called Egypt. ("And where is your home, my boy?" the Sunday School teacher enquired when the Leacock children made their first appearance. "Egypt," promptly replied the lad. "My, you have come a long way," remarked the teacher, considerably impressed. "Now tell the class where Egypt is." "A mile from Little Hell," was the unexpected answer, the latter name being that of a tiny gathering of houses presumably even more parched and arid than the one nearest to my grandfather's farm.)

Uncle Stephen took us all to the farm on a pilgrimage (pious or vengeful, I have never decided which it was intended to be), about which I will tell you in a later chapter. Further remarks about the farm will be reserved for that chapter. I mention it here, merely to help you get a clear picture of the map of Leacock Land.

The only other place on Granny's side of the lake that deserves mention was the "big house on the lake" where Granny and the younger children lived after they left the farm. I think this was "Rotherwood," a large, red-brick house with white gingerbread, which stood in a big, bare field between the Hall and Mossington's Point. My mother stayed there one summer, in a room or two she rented, when I was very small. It stood in a large bare field, and I recall our all being herded down the drive, which seemed miles long and very hot, to me, so that the village photographer could take our pictures in the shade of a big tree near the road. A memento of the occasion was a picture of my sister as a baby, still unsteady on her feet, and supported by the arms of a headless woman. Apparently my mother, feeling that she was not looking her best, asked the photographer to "cut her out," meaning to black out her image ... so he cut off her head. My only other memory of Rotherwood was of looking down through a hatch into the cellar, where a milk-snake had found its way. The reptile looked almost as long as the boa constrictors in my brothers' *Boys Own Annual*, and hideously damp, and it kept shooting its little forked tongue in and out in a terrifying fashion, making me very glad when the man who showed it to us slammed the doors shut.

If I have spent a lot of time on Granny's side of the lake, and in Granny's houses, it is because that is where Uncle Stephen came from, really; and because you cannot hope to realize what he and Old Brewery Bay are about unless you know something about Granny and her cottage and her house.

For the moment, all I will say about Uncle Stephen's house at Orillia is that there were two of them, one after the other. For he built one house bit by bit, and then he knocked it down and built another one. (The Stephen Leacock Memorial Home is the second one.) And that the same sort of hurly-burly went on over at Uncle Stephen's as at Granny's house and cottage, although not quite so hard and fast. There was the same buoyant, vibrant, happy atmosphere, the sense of the future being in the present, the same daily battle between logical theory and illogical practice, the same unbounded belief in things-as-you-want-them-to-be, and magnificent disregard of reality's shortcomings.

Beaverton, too, where they spent several summers when my uncle was young, and the girls still teenagers, I will leave till later. That will be in the chapter "The Boy He Could Not Leave Behind Him."

The last place on our tour of Leacock Land is 165 Côte des Neiges Road in Montreal. Later it was re-numbered and is now 3869. Here my uncle lived from about 1901 when he started teaching at McGill until a few years before he died. He moved to the old Windsor Hotel in about 1939, although he continued to go up to Old Brewery Bay until the summer before he died.

I think I was at this house once when I was in my teens, but cannot pin-point the year. However, when I went there in February, 1942, on my way down to Prince Edward Island to join my husband, the place looked very familiar, both outside and in.

So much then, for Leacock Land. And now let me introduce you to its people...

2

...and its People

When you look through the hedge to see my Uncle Stephen, do not think that he will be alone . . . either at Granny's place or at his own. It is almost as impossible to imagine Uncle Stephen isolated from his brothers and sisters, and his mother, as it is to imagine one part of an amoeba separate from the rest of it.

Over at Sutton he is almost certain to be talking with Granny or with Dot or Daisy or Carrie; and at his own side, there's a good chance he'll be hobnobbing with Uncle Charlie or with Uncle George. They were often at Orillia.

So let me tell you a bit about each of them. First of all I will give you a list which Aunt Dot (it looks like her handwriting) wrote out, with their initials and birthdates. I will give you full names, the names by which most people knew them. Although the girls, especially, had "christening" names fit for young duchesses, their nicknames read more like the caste of a troup of Flora-Dora girls:

Walter *Peter* Leacock (my grandfather), January 15, 1848
Agnes Emma Butler (Granny), January 8, 1844
Thomas *James* (*Jim*) Leacock, July 14, 1867
Arthur Murdock (*Dick*) Leacock, July 29, 1868
Stephen Butler Leacock, December 30, 1869
Charles John Gladstone (*Charlie*) Leacock, December 6, 1871
Agnes Arabella (*Missie*) Leacock, March 15, 1873

Edward Peter (*Teddy*) Leacock, January 6, 1875
George David Young Leacock, March 1, 1877
Caroline Theresa Frances (*Carrie*) Leacock, August 16, 1878
Maymee Douglas Leacock, November 24, 1880
Rosamond Mary Butler (*Dot*) Leacock, May 28, 1884
Margaret Lushington (*Daisy*) Leacock, September 10, 1886

A story was repeated to me of one of my Uncle Stephen's fans who was introduced to my grandmother. "You must be very proud to have so remarkable a son," she gushed. "To which of my sons are you referring?" my grandmother inquired coldly. "I have six sons and they are all remarkable."

Granny was right, too. *All* my uncles were remarkable. Although some (Uncle George, for instance) were more remarkable than others. My brothers and sister and my cousins, I am sure, felt the same way. And so did our aunts. (Unfortunately they are dead now, so they can't back me up.)

Not all of them agreed, of course, who the more-important were. Like all large families, each had her favourites. To Aunt Carrie, for example, Uncle Charlie was the most extraordinary man in the world. I recall once, after a dinner of the Stephen Leacock Associates at which she had been a guest, Aunt Carrie dropped in at the Sibbald's Shack where I was summering with my children, to tell me about the event. She was in quite a glow about it all, and repeated all the praises which had been heaped upon Stephen. Then her faced clouded, and she touched on a sore point: "Still, I don't know why they make such a fuss about Stephen, Charlie was the one! He was worth five times Stephen!" She pondered the injustice for a while. Then her face cleared and she shook her head. "I would just like to tell them how much Stephen drank," she declared. "Then they wouldn't think he was so wonderful."

THE UNCLES

Now let me tell you about my wonderful, remarkable, quite extraordinary uncles:

Uncle Jim was wonderful because he was tall and could play ragtime on the piano and smoke a cigar, all at the same time. Also because he talked through his nose, an accomplishment which I thought he had deliberately, and by zealous practice, acquired, like the piano-playing and the cigar-smoking. He wore straw boaters with loud hat-bands and a big diamond ring ("so that I can always raise $100." This familiarity with pawnshops was deliciously thrilling to us small-towners.) Uncle Jim smelled of cigars and bay rum, a combination reminiscent of my father's pipe-and-shaving-soap scent, which didn't hurt my bachelor uncle's image in my eyes.

Uncle Dick was wonderful because he, too, was tall and good-looking and had been a Royal Canadian Mounted Policeman, and had his picture taken in that uniform so that we could show him off to our playmates. (Nobody we knew in Belleville had uncles who were a spot on ours.) Eventually he outclassed the Mounties and "went into electricity," a move made by my father and the more important of my uncles back when Sir Adam Beck was electrifying Ontario. Uncle Dick invented a field coil (something which Uncle George, my father and Uncle Charlie understood, but which I don't think Uncle Stephen could). He then set up a factory in New Jersey for its manufacture, and proceeded to further glorify himself in my eyes by marrying the widow of his landlord, and having a new photo taken, sitting beside Aunt Kate, a gorgeous, full-blown Irish rose, in a touring car which looked as long as Sutton's main street. Aunt Kate was wearing a velvet hat with a brim as big as a parasol, and in the front seat was sitting my uncle's Negro chauffeur; beside the chauffeur sat Aunt Kate's white pug dog. Just try to match that for High Society! *You* don't have anything like that in your family, admit it!

Uncle Charlie was the other bachelor uncle. He was not only adored by his nieces and nephews but by generations of Sutton children, whom he took fishing and to whom he talked and listened. He was wonderful because not only did he take my brothers fishing and all of us sailing, but he knew all about ohms, amperes, watts and kilowatts, and, I gathered, was the man responsible for putting them into the tiny little wires that were strung from the high poles along the Lakeshore Road. Later, too, I learned that he had protested the Ontario Hydro's use of 25-cycle current; almost forty-five years ago, apparently, he agitated for conversion of the Niagara system to 60 cycles, protesting that the Toronto-Hamilton-Windsor district would be an isolated island of 25-current in a 60-cycle continent. As many of you know, that conversion took place in the fifties. So I was right, wasn't I, in thinking my wonderful Uncle Charlie knew more about electricity than anybody in the world? Uncle Charlie smelled of tweed, and fish and marline, which was the right sort of smell for an uncle to have.

Uncle Teddy was wonderful because he was a foreigner, living away out in Calgary, and because he had been a soldier, with shiny buttons and a swagger stick, and because my mother often stated, unequivocally, "Teddy is the funniest man in the world." Later I discovered that he made his living by mixing up several kitchen condiments, such as baking soda and the like, rolling them into little pills, putting them into small boxes labelled "Grey's Gray Caps," and selling them. Since he made enough money to give Granny very nice presents, and to drive down to Sutton quite often, I thought this was very clever.

THE AUNTS

And what about the Leacock girls, my mother and the aunts – weren't they remarkable too?

Yes, they were. They weren't exactly wonderful, because only men are *really* wonderful. (Don't you agree? Or are you a man, perhaps, and think, perversely, that only women can be really wonderful.) Still the aunts were so much better than other people's aunts, that we didn't even bother to mention it, not even among ourselves.

The Leacock aunts were almost all small (around five-foot-two) swift of brain and foot, sparkly-eyed, clever at sewing, and painting furniture, and, it should go without saying, witty. They laughed a lot, and treated us to Church-Bazaar-fish-ponds and picnics, and sent us wonderful Christmas presents from far-off places. They took us to see lovely old ladies who kept peacocks and marmalade cats, parrots and horses and doves. They were very satisfactory aunts.

Here are the individual ways in which they managed to be so exceptional, if not quite as wonderful as their brothers:

Aunt Missie (Mrs. Harry Sheppard). The oldest of my aunts died when I was a very little girl, and wasn't buried in Sibbald's Churchyard (she was a Roman Catholic), so I never knew her, not even as a bump under the Upside-Down Tree. Still, according to my mother, she was the prettiest and sweetest sister in the world. And she made an impression upon me because she married when she was very young, and had five sons and then my cousin Agnes, who was closer than a sister to me for many summers; which latter boon alone was enough to exalt Aunt Missie in my eyes.

Aunt Carrie (Mrs. Jan Ulrichsen), my godmother, and mother of Barbara, David and Dora, was a brisk as a grasshopper, and it would have been hard to say which was the livelier, her general intelligence or her wit; the latter had an acid bite to it. She had eyes even bluer than Granny's, and hair as fine as Granny's, and the colour of new gold. Strict with her own children, she seemed to us, when we were little, a little indifferent to property rights, often extending the hairbrushing or mouth-soaping of her own delinquents to Daisy's. When four of us ganged up on Mother we could often best her, but small as she was Aunt Carrie was valiant as a lion, and as thorough as a prison warden, so no one escaped when she appointed herself chastiser. Howl though we did, we admired her spirit. And busy as she must have been sewing for her own brood, she made me dresses, and doll clothes, and never forgot my birthday.

Aunt Maymee (Mrs. Henry Bergh), the quietest of the aunts, so much loved her nest of a home in Toronto that she rarely came up to the lake. We sometimes stayed overnight at her place on our way up to Granny's, a delay which we accepted in good part because Aunt Maymee lived near Riverdale Zoo, and her two sons, Harry and Teddy, would take us to see the animals. Her dining room fascinated us, because the side-board was laden with enormous silver cups which her husband, tall, handsome Uncle Henry, had won at Cambridge for rowing.

Aunt Dot (Dr. Leacock, privately Mrs. Harry Edwards). As nearly Establishment as any Leacock could be, my little doctor aunt had a more conventional sense of humour than the others, but so much heart that she was, I think, the only one whom everyone in the family adored without reservation. She and Uncle Stephen were very close, and it was she who persuaded him to see the specialist in Toronto who operated on him for cancer of the throat. As a gay young bachelor aunt, she had beautiful evening dresses and costume jewelry, which lent her a great deal of glamour in my eyes. (I recall chiffon evening dresses embroidered with scintillating beads; one, a flamingo affair with panels heavy with beads and ostrich plumes, she "handed down" to Mother, and I wept because she wouldn't let me wear it to a party; I was about thirteen at the time.) She gave dinner parties whose guests included such impressive personages as R. B. Bennett, then Prime Minister, and his friends. She drove her little car great distances, and played the piano and sang, and sent us lovely presents, always called us "dear," and was altogether perfect.

THE COUSINS

Now for the second generation – those boys and girls to whom, as my brother, Stephen, recently remarked, the great Stephen Leacock was "just another uncle."

Agnes and "the Sheppard boys" (my dead Aunt Missie's children). Agnes, first, because as I remarked earlier, she was closer than a sister to me, and, generally speaking, the inventor and ring-leader of our most exciting games. Part of her charm, for me, was that she was a Roman Catholic; this I regarded as "romantic," greatly covetting her rosary, her nonchalantly tossed-off "Hail Mary's," her incumbency at Loretta Abbey which included such "in" activities as midnight feasts in the dorms and teasing the nuns. We all daily envied her her Romanism because, while we fretted through our long morning prayers at Granny's house, Agnes played noisily outside the window, excused on the grounds that she could not conscientiously join in the Creed.

As to "the Sheppard boys," there were five of them, all much older than Agnes. The eldest, Douglas, was only eight years younger than my mother, and was like a younger uncle to all of us, teaching us how to swim and "cracking jokes" which we thought excruciatingly funny.

The Ulrichsens: Barbara, David and Dora were the "Americans" to us, living in Pittsfield, Massachusetts in winter. I recall heated arguments with Barbara as to the relative virtues of a king versus a president – arguments which were often settled by hair-pulling, scratching, and biting. Barbara was a bit older than Agnes and myself, quite tall, and rather indifferent to us three younger maidens. Agnes and I, resenting, I suppose, what we thought was her haughtiness, got back at her by mimicking her "American" accent; we felt, because of this misfortune, which she did not seem to regard as such, that she only just escaped being "common" because of her Leacock blood, with its built-in property of aristocracy.

David was a quiet little boy, who played with my brothers; and Dora, much younger than the other two, although a pretty baby, was a great drag to us, as she was often pawned off on to us to mind on rainy days. I can still remember her howls when, wanting to be off to Mossington's, the other children locked her up in the Uncle Charlie's Dog House. Engrossed in reading *Punch* and the English magazines, I stayed behind, not caring whether I was locked up all day. I don't recall even noticing "baby Dora's" howls but, when Aunt Carrie came running, I was literally, whipping boy for the absent offenders, and *my* howls could have been heard up to the Briars, I'm sure.

The Bergh boys (Aunt Maymee's children): Harry and Teddy sometimes came up to Sutton on Sunday, but owing to their mother's being such a home-body, rarely stayed overnight. We associated them with Toronto and the zoo.

Peter, Joan and Dickie (Uncle Teddy's and Aunt Gypsy's children): It was always a great event when these "foreigners" drove down from Calgary in the summer. As a toddler, Peter, according to a picture on Mother's dresser at home, had sparkly brown eyes, thick blond hair and seed-pearl teeth, assets which gave him such a head-start with me that he never outgrew it. Later, when he was attending Upper Canada College, he used to spend his Easter holidays with us in Belleville. Joan was too small to play with us, and it seems to me that Dickie was born after I had stopped going to Sutton.

Stevie: Uncle Stephen's son had a rather special position. He was both Crown Prince and Golden Boy, the child whose birth, we had been told, had been awaited for seventeen long years by Uncle Stephen and Aunt Trix. And that he should also be a boy was considered doubly miraculous. He also enjoyed a unique preciousness because he was the first of Granny's grandchildren (and she had six sons) to bear the Leacock name. The son of a son. The son of the accepted head of the family. (Uncle Stephen, having taken over the responsibility of his mother and his younger brothers and sisters when he was only sixteen, was always considered the actual head of the house despite having two older brothers.) We were almost in awe of Stevie. Later, when we went to visit him, or he was brought over to see us, we could not understand his quietness, and his unfamiliarity with the rough-and-tumble play of the other boys, but we generally humbly conceded that this must be due to some inborn superiority of the young heir.

We sent him cards and Valentines, and bought him special presents out of our Christmas allotment. I recall, when his mother died, making him a very clumsy stuffed donkey, with floppy legs cut from strips of a bicycle inner-tube.

Stephen and Dickie and Margaret and myself, Betty (Burrowes) (I shed the childish name of "Betty" when I went to University): We were Daisy's children. Stephen was Uncle Stephen's namesake (William Stephen Leacock Burrowes) and godson, and was called after him, and after my father, William Edward Burrowes.

Did you think I had forgotten about Uncle Stephen and Uncle George? Not at all. But Uncle Stephen has the next chapter to himself, and the whole book is really his, so that, I think, should content him.

As for Uncle George, I have saved him for the last, because he was so very remarkable that he deserves it, like dessert after a good meal:

Uncle George was by far the most wonderful of my uncles. Not only was he my godfather, but he could do arithmetic very fast, and was taller than any man I knew, even my father, and rode and jumped fences on enormously big horses, wearing a red coat and a black silk hat. To this glamour he added a beautiful wife with blue-black hair, creamy skin and violet eyes who also wore a black silk hat when *she* rode her little mare, Lavender, and jumped over fences. After her death Uncle George further consolidated his gains, in my eyes, by marrying an equally lovely blonde, the Aunt Mary of whom I speak in this book. Uncle George smelled of whisky, tobacco, tweed, bay rum, and horses, which amalgam, if bottled, could by virtue of its sheer devastating maleness outsell the most expensive perfume on the men's cosmetic counters of today.

Uncle George's horses, enormous brutes, were actually "outlaws" from the track, whom, he claimed, he "gentled." It is true he broke them in sufficiently for them to be shown at the Royal Winter Fair, and at the Sutton Horse Show (he was one of its founders, so this is a dubious testimony), but their rolling eyes, gnashing teeth, and frequently up-reared hooves prevented me from complete trust in my uncle's claim. I still quake when I recall Uncle George and I riding two of his hunters one morning, when we met with a horse which was being ridden by one of my uncle's neighbours. Uncle George and the neighbour were friendly enough; but their mounts did not share the affinity. I found myself suddenly atop a heaving mountain, while gazing into a mouthful of enormous teeth, as the equines prepared to settle scores. "You weren't a bit afraid, dear, were you?" marvelled my admiring uncle as we rode back to Meadowlea. I kept silent. He may well have thought my silence was due to modesty. It wasn't. I was trembling too hard to speak.

As you can see, Uncle George had, in my book, more dash than all the other uncles put together. In addition to the gorgeousness of his Hunt Club and Horse Show get-up, he wore an opera cape and high silk hat when he took me to the Royal Winter Fair, and Aunt Ethel wore a sparkly evening dress and a grey squirrel coat and pearls. And when Uncle George stopped off in Belleville to see us, he stepped right off the curb of the Belleville Front Street and lifted his cane and shouted "Taxi! Taxi!" This evidence of his sophistication left me almost speechless with pride – one phoned, an hour ahead, for taxis in Belleville at that time. Belleville let me down badly by failing to produce a cab for my uncle, and, as far as I am concerned, never did make up for this *gaucherie*.

Uncle George sent me a bright blue butterfly wing, framed, from South America; a jade and silver ring and brooch from Mexico; a white jersey with the first zipper Belleville ever saw; and scores of other wonderful, far-off-from gifts. He was, as I say, my godfather, and I named my oldest son after him (and after his father and Uncle Stephen).

Uncle George was (no matter what Mother may have felt about Uncle Teddy, or the world thinks about Uncle Stephen) the very wittiest man in creation. And if you wonder why, being so witty, he did not become famous like Uncle Stephen, I think the whole thing really depended upon the fact that he couldn't spell, and Uncle Stephen could.

3

My "not most remarkable" Uncle

If I agreed with my Granny that Uncle Stephen was not the most remarkable of her sons, it was for the same reason she advanced – that they were all remarkable. It did not mean that either I or Granny did not think *he* was wonderful. We did.

In my young eyes, Uncle Stephen was wonderful because:

Mother said so, and substantiated her statement with tales of his rescuing herself as a baby, his other younger brothers and sisters, and our dear granny from their tyrant father. This one brave deed put him away above his brothers, heroes though they had been of many boyish deeds of valour.

Granny thought so. No matter what she might say in public, Granny always looked up to and deferred to Uncle Stephen in a way which she did not do with all her sons.

He was famous, even though I did not understand why he should be. (He wrote books, a great many of them; but then I had written a book, and illustrated it, too, when I was only six or seven. At the same age my uncle was, by all accounts, frittering away his time reading and playing cricket, with no thought whatsoever of contributing to his country's literary heritage.)

Mystified though I was at the unfairness of his fame, I admired famousness, as I did beauty, intelligence, courage that was rewarded with medals, and money. So I admired my uncle for achieving fame.

... *and rich.* Even though Uncle Stephen might not advertise his wealth in the manner which I should have chosen, the fact that he made so much from his writings invested him with a kind of dazzle which was a source of great satisfaction to me.

... *and knew other rich, famous people.* People like Mary Pickford and Doug Fairbanks, Charlie Chaplin, Booth Tarkington, and other such glittering personalities, who were very much part of the smart scene in the thirties and forties.

I admired him, also, for his dinner parties and weekend house-parties, where the grown-ups laughed a lot and enjoyed themselves every minute, or so it seemed.

Uncle Stephen was remarkable because he spoke French, and joked with his friends in French, and not only lived in a French city in Canada, but wintered in the real France, across the ocean. Honesty compels me to admit that he spent only one or two winters in Biarritz; but for my purposes, his timing for the first of these sojourns could not have been better.

It was during a period when I had developed a feeling of let-down because of the lack of visible proof of my uncle's wealth. My friends at school had even become openly skeptical, pointing out that he had only one car at a time, and that he ran it for an unfashionably long number of years. Then he redeemed himself completely by taking Stevie (Aunt Trix had died a year or two before) and a small *entourage* to Biarritz.

That bit of the west coast of France was the playground of movie stars, royalty, and the more glittering literary lights; it was considered much more posh than the Riviera. To spend the whole *winter* at Biarritz . . . and at a time when, in Belleville, even bankers and stockbrokers aspired to nothing grander than two weeks at the lake in July or August! You can imagine, can't you, the *éclat* this move of my uncle's lent me among my contemporaries? I will even admit that, for a few days, I was distracted from my life-long loyalty to dear Uncle George.

Then, to cap this inspired action, Uncle Stephen brought each of his nieces a dress from France, made to each little girl's own measurements, which he had secretly secured from our parents! It is true that, in my case, the gift was a cruel come-down from what I expected. (Schooled by almost religious examination of Aunt Ethel's and some of Aunt Dot's gowns from Paris, and by equally devout study of the fashion pages of the *Ladies' Home Journal*, I had looked forward to parading a Patou or a Molyneux at the next neighbourhood birthday party. Beaded georgette and ostrich plumes, I had had in mind.) Still, woefully plain though the beautifully-made navy blue serge he sent might seem to me, at least it *had* been made in France, and made especially for me, which was more than the wealthiest of my classmates could boast.

I adored Uncle Stephen because he fished and sailed and "carpentered," all things my clever father did. I had my father's word, too, that Uncle Stephen did them well.

. . . *and because he was good-looking*, or so I thought, and had been terrifically good-looking as a young man, according to old photos.

. . . *and wore nice clothes*. Uncle Stephen's jackets and flannels might be rumpled and banged-about looking, not at all like those of my immaculate, fastidious father, but then, so were Uncle George's clothes, and Uncle Charlie's. What mattered was that they were made of the best quality tweed and flannel, and that no matter how long ago they might have come from his tailor, the tailor had obviously been a good one. Uncle Stephen's Panama might be limp and wavy as a damp sea biscuit, his tie, upon him, might resemble one of the strips of cotton with which Granny's raspberry bushes were tied up, but they were the right kind of hat, the right kind of tie.

. . . *and he smelled delicious*. Of whisky and tobacco, of tweed and fresh linen, of shaving soap, and sometimes of fish and flowers, of earth and outdoors. As did all the men of my family. If you do not recognize the smell I describe, and are a woman, I feel sorry for you. I repeat that I am fully convinced that some enterprising perfumer should bottle this stuff, call it "Eau de Leacock," and offer it on men's cosmetic counters.

... *and his house was right.* I might not like the big house at Old Brewery Bay as much as I did Granny's, but at least it had the same feel and look as the rest of the houses in my family ... easy, comfortable, totally irreverent of conventional architecture, and filled with fascinating bits and pieces of furniture and things which seemed, like those at Sutton and the cottage, and our own house at Belleville, to be almost animate. Like his clothes, my uncle's house was a natural expression of himself.

My uncle was wonderful because he had the most wonderful voice I have ever heard. It was full and sweet; not cloying, but sweet like amber-comb honey is sweet. Even in anger, it was a voice which one knew was accustomed to laughter. In it there was glory, and the consciousness of power of a man who is in control of his destiny, and knows it. It was as exquisitely shaded as a Rembrandt, but an ever-changing Rembrandt; no combination of shades, no harmony however beautiful, was ever repeated.

This was the voice of a man who could, surely, have descended from no other people but the Irish.

My uncle's accent, too, was one which I wish more linguists could hear. Particularly when I tire, as I often do, of the unquestioning reverence accorded the Oxford accent. For while Uncle Stephen spoke with an English accent, it was English-by-remove. It had some of the clarity and precision which, it seems to me, one acquires only in colder, drier climates, such as our own, or that of the Scandinavian countries. True-blue Oxford is a beautiful accent – but so was my uncle's. Hearing it you might ponder a point of view for which I find little acceptance – in my opinion, the Oxford accent is really a *local* accent, just as is the Jamaican, the

Kentuckian or the Bostonian. The educated Canadian's "English" can be just as pleasant to the ear as that of the Oxonian's; and one *accent* is as good as the other.

My uncle knew he had a good voice, and gloried in it, but his speech never appeared mechanical, studied, artificial or in any way "rhetorical" or put on. He had too good an ear for that, no matter how tired he might be. His writing might sometimes be careless and repetitive. His speech never was.

It is to me a very sad thing that even the best of the recordings of Uncle Stephen's voice capture only the ghost of its real quality. Everyone who ever heard him was fascinated by his voice; it is one of the reasons he captured and enchanted a much larger and more varied audience than one might have expected to be attracted by his writings.

He looked right at me when he spoke, even when I was very little and young; and his clear eyes reminded me of my Granny's.

... and he listened to me when I spoke to him – and really seemed to be interested in what I had to say.

... and he was kind and generous and loved us all. Not only was he generous, but he always seemed to know exactly what would most please the particular person to whom he was giving. This talent was, I later realized, one more evidence of his dedication to the belief that man, the individual, was the most important thing in the world.

Having completed this catalogue of my uncle Stephen Leacock's superiorities, as they appeared to me as a child, let me try to draw you a rough sketch of the whole man; this, partly from my adult point of view:

"What did he look like?" I am often asked now.

Like a teddybear that has been left out in the rain all spring.

Like a soldier who has fought through every battle of the Hundred Year's War.

Like a bundle of clothing ready for the St. Vincent de Paul drop-box for the poor.

Like a mischievous child, just before he bursts the paper bag full of water.

Like . . . as a gentleman who heard him lecture years ago at the Chateau Laurier told me . . . "the original hayseed. You could almost see the straw sticking out his boot-tops."

Like a safety-pin cushion, and a very old one, at that. As I have said, I never saw the famous coonskin coat which was, according to legend, held together with safety-pins; but it is certainly true that the safety-pin was as normal to my uncle's costume as buttons are to most men. Indeed, I sometimes wondered whether perhaps his tailor finished his suits with safety-pins instead of buttons. As for my uncle, I do not think he ever thought about the matter. Safety-pin, button . . . what difference did it make? Each accomplished the same purpose.

Specifically, he had grey-blue eyes that were so clear and bright you would have said they were blue; a mop of brown-grey hair which had not been told, apparently, of the invention of the comb. He had a cleft chin. And wrinkles.

Wrinkles? His face resembled a relief map of the human heart, riddled and furrowed with almost every emotion *homo sapiens* has ever experienced.

Mrs. Michelle (a daughter of the Canon Green, who unwittingly sat for Stephen Leacock's Canon Drone, in *Sunshine Sketches of a Little Town*) told me of my uncle's turning up at an Orillia funeral with his jacket fastened with the inevitable safety-pin. The bereaved family was terribly hurt, taking this touch as an indication of lack of respect for the deceased. They thought it "not very nice of Stephen," Mrs. Michelle told me.

As to Stephen Leacock's personality, it would help you to understand him if you knew that he was Irish.

It is true my uncle did not appear aware of this fact, nor did my uncles nor aunts make much of it. They considered themselves English.

Admittedly, he was born in England, as were his father and his

31

mother, perhaps even his grandfather Butler (Granny was not certain of this, according to her notes). But before that the Butlers, Granny's family, had lived in Ireland almost as long as there had been an Ireland. (Butler was the family name of the Dukes, Earls and What-Nots of Ormonde. Silly Ann Boleyn refused to marry one Butler of Ormonde who was Lord-Lieutenant of Ireland at the time.)

So what if a generation or two of Butlers, passing through, as it were, happened to be born in England? An accident, an incident. They were still Irish, I am sure you'll agree. And so was Stephen Leacock, one of the third generation of Irish transients.

If you, too, are Irish, I need say no more. For the rest of you, you have heard, have you not, of Irish word-magic, of Irish melancholy, of Irish charm? That was my Uncle Stephen . . . all of these attributes rolled into one person, but all still fighting one another, as they do in every Irishman, until the sod falls upon his coffin.

As for the Leacock side of Uncle Stephen's inheritance, there was Irish there too. I don't know how much, nor what other nationalities were in the mix. Nor do I think that it matters. After all, the Leacocks were only the father's side. I take a no-budge stand that the mother's side is the one that matters. The mother's ancestors are the determining ones. The father is just passing through, perhaps only for the few split-moments of conception. The mother, willing or not, remains, almost always, at least long enough to shape the child's life-patterns.

Not only did Stephen Leacock have the incalculable advantage of being Irish. He was also born on a Thursday. "Thursday's child is merry and glad," wrote Aunt Dot, copying out the old saw beside Uncle Stephen's name on the calendar of family births which she prepared.

Irish, and Thursday's child. There's no enigma at all to Stephen Leacock's character, is there?

4

Early Intimations

Uncle Stephen . . . Stephen Leacock . . . the famous uncle . . . was a legend long before I knew him. A far-off presence, dimly divined. Then gradually realized. And finally become flesh.

The legend began away back, before I started to school. We were living in Belleville then, in a huge white brick house which stood on the corner of Bleecker Avenue and Bridge Street East, on the edge of the town. (It was torn down many years ago, and another house built on its land.)

The Farley house (my father rented it from Major Farley who was absent in, I think, France) was a magnificent place, at least to us four children. It was really a small mansion, occupying, together with its own wooded park, a city block. It was set back on a large lawn, and had its own kitchen garden and a carriage house and stable.

Inside it had many high-ceilinged rooms, white marble fireplaces, a crystal chandelier, and a steep stair with white steps and a mahogany bannister down which Stephen and Dickie used to slide. The rooms were large, and the floors looked as vast as the Sahara desert to me, and the same colour. But they were shiny, and very slippery. I always tried to hold on to a grown-up before I crossed the floor.

Uncle Stephen was a part of the atmosphere of the Farley house. An atmosphere in which absent persons were fully as palpable as the furniture, and in which the furniture was almost as much a part of the family as the animals. Uncle Stephen; Cuff, my grandmother's long-dead horse (her mate, dead before mother's day, was called Collar); the dark Mission furniture my parents had brought with them from their North Bay and Haileybury homes; Puss, the cat; the chickens my father raised as a hobby . . . they were all there, at the Farley house, mixed up in a warm hodgepodge which gave the rented house the real aura of home. Uncle Stephen was more important, perhaps, than the little black bookcase, but not as important as the chickens, nor anywhere near as important as Puss. About on a par with Cuff, the dead horse, I should place him.

Indeed, it may have been because of some of the furniture that Uncle Stephen first achieved a separate identity for me. Because some of our furniture came from him and before that from old Henry Pellatt. I will tell you about it presently.

I must have actually seen my uncle long before Belleville, at some time when I was very small. But of the congestion of aunts, uncles, and grown-ups whom I remember, in my infant days, almost engulfing me, like a fast-running school of smelts amongst whom a minnow has wandered, only two stand out distinctly. Aunt Dot, because she made me two dresses for my third birthday (one with pink rosebuds all over it, and another with a design of raspberries and blackberries, which immediately attracted me by its "stylish" pattern. I remember I insisted on wearing this one for my birthday party; I felt, as soon as I put it on, that I had left babyhood far behind). And Uncle Teddy, who drove me to the doctor in Sutton when I broke my arm, that same summer. Uncle Stephen was, at this point, just a part of the general jumble of relatives.

At Belleville, however, the focus suddenly became sharp, chiefly because I was abruptly transplanted from Toronto, where I had been living with a friend of my mother's, to Belleville. I had been away from my family, and living among adults for a year, and had quite forgotten what children were like. From the serenity of 87 Lonsdale Road, where I lived with two quiet women, to the turbulence of family life at the Farley house was a shock which provided one of the classic conditions for recall. Strange sounds, sights, smells were received at split-second speed, everything was new. Naturally, I noticed everything. And part of everything was Uncle Stephen's furniture.

The furniture had originally come from Henry Pellatt, father of the Henry Pellatt who later became Sir, and built that architectural monstrosity known as Casa Loma. Aunt Trix, Uncle Stephen's wife was granddaughter of old Henry Pellatt, and a niece of Sir Henry's. (Her father was Colonel "Bob" Hamilton.) Whether the old man had given the furniture to Stephen and Trix as a wedding present, or whether he had sent them some of his hand-me-downs, I do not know. At any rate, Uncle Stephen and Aunt Trix had had it some years before they gave it to my parents. It must have been in their Montreal house, on Côte des Neiges Road.

There were three squarish chairs ("occasional chairs," I suppose you would call them, though "occasion" would be a better word, for, being upright, rigid and armless, they were rarely tenanted except by callers). Their light-veneered frames were decorated with a gimcrack design of shamrocks and curlicues, with the shamrocks painted green and the rest of the design black, outlined with gold. For a long time this furniture quite mystified me, because it was so unlike any other furniture I had met. (Granny's rather bashed-up walnut; my parents' Mission and wicker; the heavy carved Oriental furniture and wrought-iron beds at the Hall and the Castle.) Recently I discovered they were by Jacques and Hayes, and hence valuable Canadiana.

Curious as I was about the chairs, I didn't like them. But although the secretary was, like my father, so tall that at the Farley house I rarely saw above its base, on the rare times when I saw the upper part I loved it. This piece of furniture was walnut, and consisted of a tall, glass-doored set of shelves resting on a solid chest of drawers. A hinged shelf, lined with green felt, opened out to write upon. Immediately above it were long wells for pencils, and a square pit for an inkwell. Above it, at the base of the shelf section, were two small drawers, in which my mother kept her sealing wax, letters from Granny and her family, and at the back, the grocery bills. The doors of the secretary, however, were its glory; tall and narrow with a graceful arc at the top, and the plainest of mouldings framing the glass. This was my first acquaintance with the classic arch, and paved the way for a life-long love affair with Florentine architecture.

The secretary, incidentally, is likely up at the Stephen Leacock Memorial Home now. My mother sold it, years ago, and it was subsequently re-sold to a gentleman who presented it to the Home. My brothers have the other furniture, which is still solid and in good shape.

There was also an oval table which I thought hideous. Its shiny top was marked with swirly, pull-taffy burls, and edged with finicky beading. It had four sprawly legs and more pendants and carvings than Westminster Abbey. Still, it made a wonderful castle for my smaller dolls. There was an open cage in the centre of the pedestal where the legs met, then bulged away from each other, to unite once more in support for the top. The dark, elaborately carved inner edges of the legs made the walls of a baronial hall. From its open arches the Lord and Lady of the castle could sight visiting *entourages* from clear across the country. The visitors, tired no doubt after their long ride or walk across the broad plains of my mother's Turkish carpet, had still to clamber up the slippery spines of the table legs, which must have been very hard going, wicked as they were with knobs, beadings, frets and all sorts of pimples and woody encrustments.

While, in those early days, I grudgingly allowed the Pellatt table some practical merit, later I developed a very personal hatred of it, for it was my task, as part of my education as a housewife, to dust this bit of furniture. At best, it took half an hour to dust around all those nasty embellishments, and to lemon-oil the top till the burled veneer glistened like hore-hound taffy.

The mere massiveness of these pieces of furniture was enough, of course, to have given Uncle Stephen substance and a separate identity in the family legend. It also lent him, I now realize, a rather unfair social advantage, in that it placed him, in one move, in the sitting room. At this stage the playroom, the bedrooms, the hall and the kitchen comprised our infant scene. The dining room was associated with grown-up grandeur; still, we had our tea at a little nursery table in there before my father came home from his office, so our awe of this room was tempered by familiarity. But the sitting room was definitely out of bounds. Some times the maid took me in to be presented to tea-time callers; and I recall that the Christmas tree was in that room . . . its top so high that, straining my gaze upward, the top branches merged with the carved plaster flowers on the ceiling.

Our sitting room in the Farley house was, as I remember it, rather more magnificent than the Palace at Versailles. In fact, years later, when I visited the Sun King's palace, I found the rooms disappointingly small and ordinary. The floors looked dull and worn, after the acreages of gleaming, pale-blond wood in the Farley house. Louis XVth's Aubussons were worn and faded, while my mother's Turkish carpet had a deep shag, as rich and plushy and creamy-white as a polar bear's pelt, upon which were described dizzying hieroglyphs of scarlet, royal blue, emerald green, yellow and black. (It was these hieroglyphs which were translated into the highways, parks and mazes which the brave dolls traversed in their journeys to Pellatt Palace.) The French king's fireplaces were mostly wooden, albeit painted and decorated, while the big one in our sitting room was white marble with a huge mirror over it. His doors, too, were not as grand as the big doors that slid back into the wall; ours were white as the white bunny coat of the Archdeacon's little daughter, and very shiny; they had door knobs made of china, like my mother's teacups.

Then, too, Louis' furniture had a lot of gold on it, and even back at Bleecker Avenue, I knew that gold was "common." Silver was all right, but only if it was very old and battered up, like my Granny's teapot, or my brother Stephen's christening mug. The only gold I knew which wasn't "common" was the gold in the fillings of my father's back teeth, and in his signet ring. The fillings were all scratched and dented (he used to obligingly open his mouth very wide, so that I could feel them with my finger), and the signet ring was so old that you had to take his word for it that what looked like the very frail wings of a sea-gull were actually all that was left of the Burrowes lion.

In addition to the luxurious yet tasteful *décor* and furniture of the sitting room, there were all sorts of minor wonders from afar. There was a beaded straw belt made and worn by the Kaffirs, which Granny had brought back from South Africa; a chipped terracotta water jar somehow connected with the Black Hole of Calcutta, that came to us, by God knows what devious route, from Great-Uncle Tim (Sir Thomas Adair Butler, my Granny's half-brother, knighted for gallantry); rice paintings of birds, and carved sandalwood beads, both part of another warrior-relation's loot from the Chinese Emperor's Summer Palace, during the Boxer Rebellion. (Louis of France not only had common taste, he apparently had no adventurous or travelling uncles, for all his furnishings were new and obviously right out of a store.)

So, you see, by the simple act of sending us his cast-off furniture, Uncle Stephen stepped straight from obscurity into the upper-class, Sunday-best world of our sitting room. He established himself as a part of High Society before I had even heard the term.

Uncle George, my favourite uncle, could hold his own against Uncle Stephen by sheer personal dash and dazzle. But the manoeuvre was scarcely fair to Uncle Charlie, my dear, kind, quiet bachelor uncle, who was associated only with the Dog House behind Granny's cottage; nor to Uncle Dick, Uncle Jim, and Uncle Teddy, who were far away and had not thought to resort such ploys as the Pellatt furniture.

As far as the domestic scene went, if this association with the brilliance of the sittting room did not precisely cinch Uncle Stephen's claim to recognition, it at least elevated him to a position slightly above the chickens. He was still below Puss the cat, Cuff the horse, and Boot, my old English nurse at Haileybury. I may mention that, although he never did get the better of Puss, he left poor dear old Cuff plodding along miles behind, the day he wrote to us that he was going to spend the winter in Biarritz.

Uncle Stephen gave us the living-room furniture and he also gave us wonderful Christmas gifts. Especially to my brother Stephen, who was his godson. (I remember thinking how strange it was that this uncle whom I had never seen should have the same name as my brother; Saint Stephen was his only namesake, as far as I had known up to that point.)

That Christmas at the Farley House was the first one upon which I can remember realizing that not all our presents came from Santa Claus, and that the whole amazing, mind-boggling affair was actually an adult co-op effort. Under the Farley House Christmas tree were presents from Granny, from Aunt Carrie and Aunt Dot, from cousins as small as ourselves, and from a brace of uncles. I cannot remember what Uncle Stephen sent any of us except Stephen, and he got a book, with his name written in the front, and a tool-box with a real hammer, just like my father's.

Stephen's parcel came separately, with his own name on it. Letters from the relations were always a terrific event to us, still foreigners in Belleville and feeling as homesick for Granny's Lake and the familiar faces as the child Stephen Leacock did for Portchester and Hambledon. We used to swing on the front gate, waiting for the postman, and before we handed the letters to our mother we had "read" the handwriting to see who had sent them: Granny's thin, runaway hand; Uncle George's huge uninhibited scrawl; the Chinese puzzle of Aunt Carrie's spidery hieroglyphics. Of all these, Uncle Stephen's broad, strong, black script had the distinction of being legible, even to a child. The "l's" were always closed, the "i's" were dotted, the name "Stephen" quite recognizable.

Most children are mercenary, I suppose, and the adult with the open hand, the dispenser of largess, will not go unnoticed. It is not that the recipient necessarily appreciates the donor's generous disposition; he simply marks him out as a source of supply. The purpose of the kitchen tap is to quench thirst; of the chickens to provide eggs; of the baker boy to deliver bread; *ergo*, the giver gives. It is worth remembering such a person, no matter for whom you may reserve your heart.

As I have already said, Uncle Stephen had a wonderful way with gifts. He knew just when to give and what to give. He had a great sense of what was important to one, particularly to children. My mother, writing of the big brother she knew back at the farm recalled the part he used to play in the younger children's Christmases. "He used to bring Dot and me wonderful toys from 'town' (Toronto). He loved Christmas and in later years he would have us hang up pillow slips instead of stockings. 'Stockings aren't half big enough' he'd say. If the pillow slips were only half-full we never noticed. All we were aware of was the excitement, Christmas morning, of delving into them to see what we'd got."

Mother continues, "I . . . remember one Christmas at the farm. Dot was six and I was four. Stephen got Dot skates and after breakfast we went down to the pond, and Stephen took a kitchen chair and had Dot push it about to learn to skate."

When we were at the Farley House, my uncle sent my brother his first real suit . . . a terrific thing to do for a little boy. It must have been when Stephen was about six, and I don't believe it was a birthday present. I think my uncle simply realized that a boy of six yearns to put away his childish short trousers and sweater, his cotton little-boy suits, and yearns for a suit like his father's. My uncle must have sent to my mother for Stephen's measurements, and I think the suit was tailor-made . . . a wonderfully sophisticated costume of grey tweed, with a Norfolk jacket and knickerbockers.

When Stephen put it on, together with the shirt and tie, the black stockings and lace boots that went with it, we were so in awe of him that it was days before Dickie resumed his murderous attacks upon his older but frailer sibling; as for me, I immediately reverted to the tongue-tied state into which my reunion with the other children had flung me several months before. It seemed impossible that this suave, elegantly-tailored young man of the world could be the same boy who had come crying to mother with a cut and grubby knee only a few days before. An enormous gulf separated William Stephen Leacock Burrowes from us babes in nursery pinafores, or stove-pipe pants and jersey.

For many years my uncle used to send my mother $25.00 each Christmas, well ahead of the date, so that she could shop for his gifts for the other three children, and for her own. I am pretty certain that the $25.00, which was an enormous sum in those days, the equivalent of about $100 today, provided a great many other goodies besides the toys she tagged, "From Uncle Stephen."

Close after the arrival of the cheque from Uncle Stephen, came a huge hamper from England (plum puddings, dark, wine-soaked Christmas cake, books in which knights and teddybears were heroes, doll's clothes from Cousin Maymee Douglas' Church Bazaar). It was as if my uncle triggered the start for all the other Christmas preparations. And, indeed, he likely did. Particularly since times were not so easy for us then, in spite of the splendours of our house. The year before we moved to Belleville, my father's business partner had walked out with the company's total monies. My father never completely recovered financially from this disaster, and it is quite possible that my poor, hard-pressed mother could not have added Christmas extras to her grocery bill, which, like the National Debt, seemed to multiply itself each year. So we had many reasons to be grateful to Uncle Stephen for his Christmas munificence.

There was a period in my early youth when I also believed that Uncle Stephen actually was French. I came upon this piece of knowledge when, observing the funny little roof over the "o" of Côte des Neige, on one of Uncle Stephen's letters, my mother told me that the word was French. It was then that she also explained that the city he lived in was French, and that he not only wrote the language, but he spoke it as well. Since I was too young to understand the niceties of a person being able to speak more than one language, I promptly assumed Uncle Stephen was a Frenchman. As a result he immediately acquired some of the dazzle attached to Marie Antoinette's husband, and all the other Louis.

I nearly foundered over this disclosure, and over the fact that Uncle Stephen should have another home, and in a French city to boot. (Even though it was only Quebec French, as I discovered later.) My uncles were a summer phenomenon. They were part and parcel of Granny's Lake, like Bovair the liveryman, and Hannah and Lottie, the Indian women who brought us each a little birchbark canoe at the beginning of summer. Even Uncle Teddy and Uncle Jim, who did not live at Granny's Lake, were part of the summer scene as far as we were concerned. And Uncle Stephen was part of the lake, even though he didn't live at Granny's cottage or Granny's house, but in his own house on the other side of the lake.

The idea that he should have another home, just for winter, and in a city where the people spoke with roofs over the "o's" and funny little slanty sticks on other letters ... well, you can see why, all in all, I thought he had it away over the French kings, who, as far as I knew might be French, but had no English-speaking summer homes. I can tell you, Puss and Uncle George had a close call the day I found out Uncle Stephen was French; only long-established loyalty prevented me from demoting them.

At the same time that Uncle Stephen began to separate himself from the general family legend and acquire an identity of his own, we also began to notice something else very unusual about him. Something that people outside our private fence appeared already to know. He was famous.

And this was true, of course. Stephen Leacock was famous to the world even before we had granted him a chair of his own, so to speak. His name was always cropping up when my mother's new acquaintances came to call. When this happened my mother assumed a rather special manner, very offhand, while at the same time quietly important. It was the deportment of a democratic duchess, I later thought ... not openly condescending, but still conscious of her superiority. I was too little to understand what was being said and eavesdroppers were severly dealt with, so I grasped little except that the ladies always grew especially animated and gushy at the name "Stephen Leacock"; and after they were gone my mother would hum a song to herself, or look very pleased and pensive, and I was quite likely to be given a coconut macaroon, or a piece of thin, buttered, currant bread before she rang for the maid to take away the tea tray.

If, on the rare occasions when I was walking with my mother on the street, and she fell into conversation with another lady, and the exciting name was again bantered, the outcome was quite different from the times when his absent person was lionized in our home. For now, as soon as the passerby was out of earshot, my mother would become unaccountably critical. "Betty, don't chew the elastic of your hat!" or "You shouldn't look down when people speak to you." It was of the earliest instances of my feeling that Uncle Stephen had in some way degraded me in my mother's eyes. The vague sense of grievance ... my first realization of a mixed attitude toward any one grown-up ... was intensified when we approached school age, and were considered old enough to go beyond our house and our woods. For Uncle Stephen, in becoming famous, had thrust fame upon us. And we were in no way up to it.

A common experience, at this stage, was being stopped on the street by adults, generally females, both because they were at large at the same hours as we were, and because, I suppose, literary lions are the particular pets of the sensitive sex. Imagine us coming home from Haines Grocery Store, for instance, totally preoccupied with deriving every demi-ounce of flavour from our all-day suckers. (At that time, a "sucker," as lollipops were called, cost one cent, the sum total of each child's weekly allowance.) You can imagine how little we would wish to be distracted from this orgy, whose sensual content it would be difficult to surpass. Two ladies, in tea-party hats, would recognize us (this became easier and easier, as our connection with Stephen Leacock was bruited up and down Bridge Street East). Then would follow the arrest, the questioning. All of it, for a long time, quite incomprehensible to us. Why weren't other children stopped? Why did these adults ... generally strangers to us ... single us out?

The general line of interrogation was pretty much the same every time. What were our names? Where did we live? Later, after we had started to school, what did we like best at school? This was often put in the form of a leading question, "Do you like Composition?" At our academic level, Composition, in those days, could only mean English Composition, and the expected answer was an enthusiastic "yes." Our inquisitors must have been thrown, I am sure, by the inevitable "no," with which Stephen and Dickie and

I replied. To young students of the Ontario schools at that time, English Composition was a peculiar exercise in which a child, who had no difficulty in sharing his dream of going around the world in a ship of his own making, or killing a brace of lions, or (ermine robe clad, of course, with a golden crown upon her royal head) righting all the wrongs of the world, was asked to imagine itself a postage stamp, or a rubber ball, or an old shoe. We did not like composition.

Much later, looking back, I realize that what my uncle's fans in Belleville were fishing for was my brother's name, and the information, clearly and concisely stated, that it was *his* ambition to become a famous writer. I recall having some dim inkling that Stephen was the one in whom they were most interested. (The ladies smiled at one another, and sometimes at him, with particular fatuity.) But then, I thought that was only his just due, as a male, and our leader. Looking back, I believe Stephen should have exercised more discretion. If he had to say his Christian name, when asked, could he not at least, have concealed the famous surname which had been bestowed upon him in honour of his godfather? Once, not content with his answer "Stephen," to the classic question "What's your name?" one of our star-struck neighbours had persisted, "And what is your other name?" Had my brother realized that the question was a trap, surely he could have satisfied himself by replying, "Stephen Burrowes." But no, Stephen, to whom guile was always impossible and still is, answered with his whole name: "William Stephen Leacock Burrowes." I cannot wholly blame my brother, of course, for we were all, at this stage, completely mystified as to why so much attention was being paid us. Still, this indiscreet disclosure likely did a lot to aggravate the discomforts of premature fame. The legend was moving in upon us. . . .

5

Legend Becomes Flesh

Memory, like a poorly edited film, jumps and backtracks. We cannot be sure that the sequence of shots is historically true; or, if convincing chronologically, it strikes us as artistically false. Frames are frozen which appear to have no importance to the viewer, while other scenes flick past so fast we cannot identify the actors.

So now, when I try to fix a time and a place where the legend that was Uncle Stephen became flesh, what turns up? A boxful of faded cracked old film, brittle with time, threatening to split into useless little bits if I handle it carelessly. Hundreds of feet in which I search in vain for the Man in the Panama Hat. (Granny is there, little Stevie is there, Freddy Pellatt is there . . . but where is Uncle Stephen?) He appears in much footage, but not at the period I am looking for. It is the beginning of the story for which I search, the Enter-Our-Hero sequence.

Let us keep to the oldest footage. Most of it faded, much of it so brittle it is ready to break; but every now and then I come across a length in which the image is sharp and clear, the voices as distinct as if they had been recorded in a sound-proof studio.
Sort them out, set aside only those in which The Man appears.
What have we now? Let us catalogue it:

    Whistle-Stop Sequence
    Corkscrew Sequence

Birthday Party Sequence
Pilgrimage to Egypt Sequence
Jesuit Priest Sequence
Argument with Granny Sequence
Assortment of Sutton Sequences
Old Brewery Bay Sequence I
Old Brewery Bay Sequence II
Old Brewery Bay Sequence III
Assortment of Old Brewery Bay Sequences
Assortment of unidentified Sequences

Let us run it through the projector. Why don't you go out in the lobby and talk with your friends while I see what's here? But don't let me take too long. You know how people are with family albums; at least, with old snapshots of their own family. They'll pore over them for hours, if you'll let them. You'll have a hard time yanking them back to the present if you leave them at it too long.

For my part, too long a time in the viewing room gives me a headache. I blink like a mole when I come back out into the sunlight, and am abstracted and vague. So, in your interests and mine, don't give me too much time. Specify the time it takes for you to smoke one cigarette, to drink one coke. Then I'll try to be businesslike and keep to the job in hand. See you in fifteen minutes time.

Now I have it for you, the early Man-in-Panama-Hat sequences. I have saved only the footage where The Man's image is clear, and the action definite. The sound track is not always what I would wish, but what can one expect of film as old as this? The camera work (was it Douglas Sheppard's? Granny always said he was "clever with a camera") is better than the sound recording.

Just look how much footage I had to discard. Practically all of it Enter-Man or Exit-Man; so many Entrances and so many Exits, with all the middle of the sequences missing.

Where did we, the children go, while the grown-ups talked, that I can remember nothing but Uncle Stephen arriving and

Uncle Stephen leaving? If it had been Uncle George, who, as soon as he arrived, started paying out what he termed "the toll" ... nickels, dimes, quarters, once even a whole dollar to each child ... we would have hurried over to Laviolette's for double ice-cream cones, or to Pivnick's for toys. But Uncle Stephen never gave us money. Wonderful Christmas presents, superb surprises on occasions not every relation remembered as special. But no hand-outs.

Perhaps, of course we scattered in self-protection, to avoid the dubious blessing of his latest benevolence. (I am thinking, for example, of the birthday party in the bush, and the pilgrimage to Egypt.) At Sutton it would be down the riverbank for the boys, behind the raspberry patch for the girls. At the cottage it would be into the sand caves, of course. I have a lot more entrances in this boxful of discards than I have of exits, so maybe we fled even further afield, to the Rectory, or well along the riverbank, if the scene was one at Sutton; at the lake, we would have disappeared towards Mossington's Boathouse, or under the culvert opposite the Briars.

Just for documentary interest, glance over some of these entrances; enter Uncle Stephen in the MacLaughlin, the car head-on through the big wire gate of the cedar hedge at the cottage; the driver (Freddy Pellatt?) serious and intent upon braking the car, Uncle Stephen's face, smiling broadly, dimly discerned over his shoulder; the car door opening, Uncle Stephen's hand setting his Panama back upon his head.

Another taken at the cottage: Uncle Stephen coming, on foot, through the tall cedar trees (once a hedge, which no one had thought to discourage) that screen the lane behind the cottage from the lawn; the MacLaughlin in the background, still chortling and shimmying with relief at having got the trip over with, the driver at the dash board; Uncle Stephen calling out, "Carrie! Daisy! Where are the children?" (Was I so small he didn't notice me, or didn't I count? Likely not. The boys seemed to me to be the only ones that counted with Uncle Stephen, back then; and Agnes, who was bold and daring as a boy, in spite of her long amber-blond hair and her blue, soot-lashed eyes.)

Again, zoom in on the cottage verandah, with Uncle Stephen stepping up on to it from the left side of the frame. His pipe is in his hand, and his cane hooked over his arm; you can just hear the car, subsiding into chuckles, "Daisy! Where are Stephen and Dickie? Carrie, where's Barbara? How is Jan? What do you hear from Billie, Daisy?"

More, so many more Enter-at-Cottage scenes. And here are the Exits-from-Cottage: Uncle Stephen climbing back into the car. Uncle Stephen looking back through the oblong isinglass window in the rear of the car as it goes out through the big wire gate. Uncle Stephen leaning down to kiss goodbye to Granny, who is sitting in her camp-chair, the Panama in his hand, putting his hat back on, and disappearing off left.

And almost as many Enter-at-Bury-Lodge scenes. Same car, same uncle, but instead of the cedar hedge the parched plain of the Sutton "lawn," the big, greyish-white stucco block of the house, fringed at the bottom with hideous pink and liver-coloured hollyhocks, lying spang ahead of the camera. Here we see the car rounding the "circular drive" (the diameter must have been all of 15 feet; I wonder that the MacLaughlin did not break its back trying to maneouvre it). The sound track records the crunch of gravel, and a tinny "ping" as a stone hit the undercarriage. I do not know whether Granny's drive was freshly gravelled each season, or whether it did not get enough traffic to round the edges of the stones, but they were very white and sharp as flints. We were not allowed to go barefoot at Sutton; as Uncle Stephen explained in *The Boy I Left Behind Me*, "In summer the (neighbour) boys went barefoot. We didn't . . . a question of caste and thistles." There were no thistles at Bury Lodge, but caste was as persuasive an argument as ever with Granny against our discarding our sandals and sneakers. However, even if shoes had not been *de rigeur*, our naked soles could not have taken the drive at Granny's, spoiled as they were by the silky-textured sand of the cottage lane, and the Hall drive, whose gravel had been worn smooth by more than a century of Sibbald feet (shod, of course; they were gentry feet, like the Leacock's) and Sibbald carriage and car wheels.

Still, the stones of Granny's drive could be felt even through our sandal soles. As a result, we generally walked along the edge of the drive, as there was no provision for the passage of pedestrians. The grass was coarse and generally dried, not at all like the soft-as-hair greenery at the cottage, but it was a lot better than the flinty driveway.

Another Bury Lodge Entrance reveals Uncle Stephen coming around the house to the lawn on the Rectory side; Granny is looking up and smiling, and reaching for her canes, hooked over the back of the cedar chair; Mother reaches anxiously for the teapot (God knows why; Uncle Stephen was not an afternoon tea-drinker, but it was a gesture as habitual with her as a nun fingering her beads, or a mediaeval man clasping his dagger).

Here, again at Sutton: Uncle Stephen coming into the narrow hallway, calling, as he comes through the door, "Mother! Where are you, Mother?"; and Granny's voice, from her bedroom "Just a minute, Stephen. Is Stevie with you?"

This, too, at Sutton: Exit Uncle Stephen, carrying Stevie in his arms, and the driver putting a big picnic basket on the floor of the car. Again, exit Uncle Stephen, very fast, through the front door at Bury Lodge, his face very closed-in looking and not at all smiling; and Granny watching him through the door, and looking sad. (Oh dear, I do remember that day, but not all of it, because I was sent into the sitting-room when Uncle Stephen's voice became so loud that I could hear it through the closed door of Granny's room. Afterwards I figured out that must have been the time that Granny told him she didn't like his last book, that he was writing too much and too fast.)

So many Entrances and Exits, without any middle action. But they give you an idea of how often he came over to our side of the lake, and with what little warning.

Of all this early footage, the only sequences worth salvaging are: The Whistle-Stop at Belleville; The Corkscrew Sequence; the three Old Brewery Bay Sequences; The Pilgrimage to Egypt; and the Birthday Party in the Bush.

I am not at all sure of their actual historical order, except for the Whistle-Stop Sequence, which I know was first. All the Old Brewery Bay Sequences are made up of a lot of short footages, spliced together. I have sandwiched the Birthday Party Sequence in between them for the sake of action. I put the Corkscrew Sequence in after Whistle-Stop for the same reason, although in actual fact, it must have been about the same time as the Pilgrimage to Egypt and the Birthday Party.

So let the projector roll.

FADE IN, through a cloud of steam on
A WHISTLE-STOP IN BELLEVILLE
when, one winter day, the legend that was my famous uncle, Stephen Leacock, became visible.

But only up to the knees.

Like Elijah, he descended from the clouds in a chariot.

The chariot was, to be exact, a CNR Pullman car. His descent was from its steps to the platform of the North Belleville train station; and the clouds were clouds of steam.

Whether they were actually so dense that they hid my uncle from me, or whether, struck by the awesome spectacle of the towering black engine, fidgetting its pistons and huffing importantly, I had only eyes for it, I do not know. However it was, this was the only opportunity I ever had to verify the existence of the legendary coonskin coat. And I cannot say whether or not he was wearing it. All I can remember was a hard-looking felt hat (a fedora, I suppose), and a general impression of dark grey tweed.

We were living at the Farley house when we went up to the station to see my uncle, on his way either to or from Toronto. (It seems to me the train was pointing toward Toronto, so I suppose he must have been on his way to a lecture.) I remember mother's excitement, and that either the train was early or we were late, for it was in the station when we arrived, and he was standing in the doorway of the Pullman. I am pretty certain he was alone; I am sure I would have remembered Aunt Trix, if she had been with him. What seems to me strange now is that there were no reporters at the station, for he was at the height of his fame then

— and big news. This makes me think that my uncle could not have given my mother much notice that he would be going through. She would not have notified the newspaper, of course, but she would certainly have told the maid, and from then on the grapevine would surely have carried this tid-bit to the press.

On so historic an occasion as this, I should, of course, be able to recall what my uncle said to me, or at least to one of the others. But I don't. All that comes back to me is being rushed out of the taxi and tugged along too fast for my legs toward the train. Then of Mother talking to the cloud of steam. I suppose their voices were drowned out by the noise of the train, or maybe he didn't speak directly to us. I am not even sure that at the time, I knew that this was the famous uncle; I do not remember any feeling of curiosity about him or interest, so we must then disappointingly FADE OUT again on the baggy tweed knees and the fedora, forever enveloped in steam.

The bell clangs, the conductor calls "All Abo-o-oard!," the pistons start to grind, more steam rises from the vicinity of the wheels, the train slowly moves toward Toronto. The children, heads not nearly up to the level of the shovelled-back snowdrifts, obediently wave their mittened hands toward the steam, from which the face emerges clearly for the first time . . . looking very like Uncle Charlie, a bit like dimly-remembered Uncle Teddy-in-Calgary, a little like Uncle George, the same blue-grey eyes looking directly out from the relief-map flesh, the same crinkles at the corners of the eyes, the same finger-deep furrows on the brow, the same shredded wheat hair beneath the fedora brim, the same teddybear-fur eyebrows, the same carelessly got-together neck gear. The famous uncle smiles, the lips move in farewell, a clumsily gloved hand waves. We keep on looking at the train; we have still a confused feeling that we have come up to see the train, that the uncle is only incidental. I know my mother must have looked after the train, sending herself with it as far as she could go. Then she said, automatically, "Take the Ketsie's hand, Stephen; come along Dickie." And, with the baby in her arms and Dickie in tow, and Stephen dutifully leading me, we disappear off-scene.

6

The Corkscrew Sequence

The scene was Granny's cottage, at the lake, but Granny was not there. I do not need to strain my memory to recall this. I am certain that the scene would never have taken place if Granny had been at the cottage. The famous man might awe bankers and members of Parliament, might indulge in shows of temperament before the public; the kindly husband and father might occasionally turn cruel dictator and shout in his own house – but in Agnes Emma's presence, he would never have dared to show his temper.

That day, however, the benevolent uncle turned ogre, and I was at the receiving end of his temper. It was the only time I was present when he lost his temper, although later, when my sister stayed with him, and through remarks from other cousins and my mother, I came to realize that it is not always fun to live near a funny man, that a humorist may sometimes be a man of bad humours too.

I asked Stevie, my cousin, about his tempers recently. "Oh, yes, indeed he had a temper," agreed his son. "But then, what would you expect? A man who is given to high spirits and great elations, naturally experiences the reverse. Just as he was way up when he was up, so he was away down when he was down." But, according to Stevie, his father was rarely depressed for long. A swift and often terrible burst of temper, and the bad mood was over. He was, essentially, a happy man, and in control of himself.

He was happy enough at the beginning of the corkscrew episode. I was just finishing dressing, after my swim, when I heard footsteps on the verandah, and the familiar voice. "Daisy! Daisy! Where are you?" he cried as he rounded the corner from the lawn. Mother was indoors, or perhaps down at the lake. At any rate I was the only person in sight. My uncle advanced swiftly down the verandah, with Freddy Pellatt or whoever was driving for him that day (I cannot remember who it was) following him, carrying a large carton.

"Daisy? Daisy!" Uncle Stephen called again, the comb-honey voice a bit more comb than honey as he grew impatient. Then as she still did not appear, he called, "Betty! Get me a bottle opener from the kitchen."

With only the haziest idea of what a bottle opener was ("Pop" being "common" was never imbibed in our house or at Granny's, and the traditional brew of raspberry vinegar was served in glasses) I hastened toward the kitchen. Eager to serve the great man I rummaged in the kitchen table drawer, anxious to find the bottle opener before Gladys, the maid, beat me to it, and deprived me of my moment of importance. Her bedroom door, which led into the kitchen, opened just as I sped back to my uncle. Proudly I tendered the instrument into his outstretched hand.

Uncle Stephen looked at the tool. Then he looked at me. His face began to get pink, then red. There was no laughter in the blue-gray eyes now. Only ice and a stillness like lake-water in winter. Then my uncle spoke, in a very distinct, determinedly level voice, "Betty, this is not a bottle opener. It is a *corkscrew*," and he threw the corkscrew the full length of the verandah.

"Now, Betty," he said, still speaking very clearly, but in a voice which ascended rapidly to a roar which I thought must split his throat, "go to the kitchen and get me *a beer bottle opener!*"

Then he turned to my mother, who had come hurrying at the sound of his upraised voice. "Daisy," he said, 'you have raised an idiot."

At this point I fled. But from indoors, where I finished my dressing as fast as I could, in order to escape the whole terrifying scene,

I could hear Mother and Uncle Stephen locked in a verbal battle of frightful ferocity. My mother adored my uncle, and, on principle, would generally have sold any of us out shamelessly, agreeing in her heart of hearts that all of us, especially me, were poor things intellectually compared to her hero. Still, something more than maternal pride was at stake this time. The issue was Temperance.

For my mother was a most intemperate advocate of temperance. Not that she was a blood-and-thunder salvationist. (Actually, I had the impression that she thought Carrie Nation and her hatchet-wielding disciples rather middle-class.) Mother was Scientific. Christian Scientific. Mary Baker Eddy, the lady-like, well-educated Bostonian, was her preceptress. "Man is not corporeal, he is spiritual," we parroted each night as we recited Mrs. Eddy's "Scientific Statement of Being" before our shorter, homemade prayer.

As Mother construed the Bostonian's teachings, man did not need food, clothing, aspirin tablets, vaccine or even raspberry vinegar, let alone Crown Royal. By lumping alcohol with roast beef and vaccine, Daisy neatly sidestepped the stigma of appearing to regard its consumption as immoral. Such a point of view was one with that of the Seventh Day Adventists and the Baptists and other such working-class religions, and therefore "common." Proper descendant of a Church of England clergyman that she was, my mother would have regarded such policing of one's personal morals "in poor taste." By claiming science as her patron saint, she managed to stay in the right club, and even to one-up the Church of England intellectually.

Actually, Mother added to Mrs. Eddy's calm "scientific" statements her own personal interpretation of the Bible, Granny's moral views, and various bits and pieces of social theory she had picked up *en route*. All this was woven into a religious viewpoint of such strong conviction that it could not be shaken by all the logic of Solomon, the pleadings of my father and her family nor any amount of trial. I am sure that the temperance bit harked back to early tales she had heard, from her older sisters and brothers, of her drunken father.

Mind you, temperance to Daisy did not mean, don't drink too much. It meant don't drink any alcoholic beverage. Drink included not only whisky but beer and wine. I later wondered how a woman who so disapproved of alcohol could reconcile herself to accepting a legacy from her father's family, whose fortune had been founded on their vineyards in Madeira. Or, for that matter, what she did about the fact that her own dear mother drank wine and, as I mentioned earlier, brewed a dandelion wine which was almost as heady as whisky. At any rate, although Mother imbibed most intemperate draughts of tea, and on hot summer days, mixed gallons of raspberry vinegar which quite often had a wicked zing to it (she was firmer on the theory of alcohol than on the mechanics of its manufacture), she also fought valiantly against Drink. She lectured anyone who would listen on its evil effects. (Beating wives and children among the lower classes; beating servants and horses among the aristocrats; and general deterioration of the brain and body, although why this should matter, if man did not really have a body, only Mother could explain.) As all of my uncles except Uncle Charlie drank (he drank beer, but not very often in her presence), and several of my aunts, and her Sibbald friends, Daisy had a busy time of it trying to set them right. When Uncle George, a volatile man always, lost his temper at her haranguing, she was delighted. It proved her point. His natural outburst became a "drunken temper," on a par with the brutal fury of the coachman in Black Beauty who beat poor Ginger so mercilessly.

But if Daisy was all out for Prohibition, Uncle Stephen was fighting the cause tooth and nail, both for the sake of principle and for self-preservation. I believe it was several years after the corkscrew argument that, not content with reasoning with my uncle when they met, my mother actually conducted a direct mail campaign against his personal intemperance.

Most certainly, she argued with him that day mostly intemperately; and I should imagine that Uncle Stephen must have swallowed several cool beers before his good humour was restored. To run head-on into an imbecile niece on boiling summer day was trying enough, but to be scolded for drunkenness before he had even begun to slake his thirst, must have been indeed hard to take. Upon mature reflection I think he was most temperate. He should have thrown the corkscrew at me, not the floor.

7

The House at Old Brewery Bay

Stephen Leacock's house at Old Brewery Bay was a large, very beautiful, white-walled villa whose top floors were given over to several spacious, well-appointed guest rooms, each with its own bath. Set on broad, velvety lawns, it looked out through leafy boughs, upon the sapphire waters of Lake Couchiching. Here one might swim in the quiet cove near the house, sail or fish on the lake in the owner's yacht, or happily stroll among the gardens and through the verdant forest.

My uncle's house at Old Brewery Bay was a big, ill-proportioned two-storey structure imperfectly clad in greyish stucco, and housing on its upper floors a collection of iron hospital beds and white enamel basins which were oddly stained with brown. (I say oddly, because how can a basin become rust-stained from whose taps water never flows?) Another interesting feature was the dense army of mosquitoes, unequalled in size and ferocity by any other animal save perhaps the tigers of Bengal. The house was set in an untamed wilderness of burnt grass and trees of uninteresting species. It overlooked a narrow tarn whose murky waters concealed perilous trapworks of bone-brittle, long-dead tree branches. Children, not yet old enough to realize the inadvisability of bathing in these waters, might have been warned, too, against going aboard in the small covered dinghy which served the host for fishing and excursions on the outer waters. It was the habit of the owner to consign the younger crew below decks. Since the hold was small, and the voyage often lasted several hours, suffocation was a risk, as was starvation, the ship's diet not being, as a rule, suited to young stomachs.

Same house, same bay, same boat. The only difference is in the point of view . . . Uncle Stephen's (as given in Description A), or mine (as given in Description B).

It is only fair to remark that my point of view was that of a child, and an unwilling guest; and that the host's idea of his home was shared by most adults. ("I remember the lawn was always dried up, and there were no flowers to speak of," I remarked to my cousin Barbara recently. "It must have been a bad summer," Barbara promptly rejoined. "The garden was always lovely when I was there.") Orillians, too, speak of it as "a beautiful old place." Fairness also compels met to admit that, just as pride of ownership gilded my uncle's impressions of his home, so did comparison with Granny's cottage militate against it in my eyes.

Incidentally, we did not call the place Old Brewery Bay when we were children; it was simply "Uncle Stephen's House." As I explained in an earlier chapter, there were actually two successive houses. The first house, which was set a little nearer to the lake, was torn down before Uncle Stephen built the place which now, as the Stephen Leacock Memorial Home, is the object of pious pilgrimage.

To be more exact, there was one-plus-plus-plus house before the present one, for the first one appears to have been self-propagating, shooting out extra wings, bulging into more rooms, like an ambitious amoeba, until in its final, pre-destroyed form it was almost as large as the present dwelling.

My mother has described how Uncle Stephen built the first house. This account has been published in other books, and brochures, so if you have already read it, just skip the following insert:

> The spot he picked was in a sheltered bay and the Old Brewery, from which the house got its name, was at the South end of this bay.
>
> There was great activity that first Summer when Stephen and Charlie built the one roomed cottage – "cook house" they

called it, and we used tents for sleeping. The year following they built a large verandah, partly closed in across the front with two small bedrooms leading off it at either end, and the kitchen at the back of it. In the verandah sitting room Stephen put a Franklin stove. One Fall, some time later, my husband and I were staying at Stephen's and he showed us with great pride how he had built an asbestos fireplace and chimney to conceal the iron body of the stove. It was very effective – a red front and a dark chimney. He had painted the asbestos in red and black and marked it off to look like bricks. "Just wait till you see it going" he said as he lighted it. The little open front did look like a real grate fire. We admired and enjoyed it, when suddenly a flame shot out from the chimney and then another. Fortunately with the lake only a few feet away, a quickly formed "bucket brigade" had the fire under control. Stephen's only comment was "too bad – still it really worked." It certainly did.

In the following years, bigger and better rooms were built, but that first little "cook house" was still in the centre of the house. The sitting room, dining room, big kitchen and guest rooms were like arms flung out and around it. Later on it was hard to realize that the pretty children's dining room had started out as a "cook house."

Whatever I may have felt about subsequent visits and the house that now stands on Old Brewery Bay, I remember that I liked the first house. It was long and low, with Aunt Trix's and Uncle Stephen's bedroom at the front, opening, as I recall, on the verandah. Leading off this bedroom, or across a narrow hall from it was Stevie's nursery; it, too, opened on the verandah, and one could see the lake from there. Looking back, I realize that quite likely one reason I preferred the first house was its proximity to the water.

I cannot remember all the rooms in the house, nor the plan. I can see now, after reading Mother's description of the way this first house evolved, that my confusion was not entirely due to the fact that I was very young when I was first visiting there. As she says,

"The original cook house became the pretty children's dining room," and no doubt former bedrooms became sitting rooms and so forth. No wonder I had difficulty orienting to the house when I came over from Sutton. It was not only that it was not laid out the same as Granny's cottage, but that it was not laid out even the same as itself — or at least the self of the summer before last.

I do remember a long gallery at the back of the house, and I think the children's dining room was at the kitchen end of this. At any rate, we ate at the kitchen end of it. I loved this gallery. It had a floor of real red tile. (So did the present house, originally, but these had had to be replaced with, I believe, red cement.) By "real tile" I mean terracotta clay, like the tile one finds in Mexico, not the ersatz, plastic stuff which is the only tile many of my younger readers will know. The roof had tiles of the same colour. This was my first experience with this delicious shade of red. Red to me had always meant Santa Claus red (early rejected for its screaming intensity); vermilion, which mixed very satisfactorily with water; carmine, all right in a paint box, but streaky when mixed; and scarlet. Maroon I disliked so much that I tried not to think about it, let alone use it.

But the tiles on the floor and on the roof were a wonderful shade. Warm and almost golden in sunlight, they became, when rained upon, very shiny, and an even more "solid" colour.

I was fascinated with this floor, and used to sit on the edge and stroke the tiles (they were very warm and smooth), and poke at the red dust which had collected along the broken edges of some tile, marvelling to find that each tiny grain and piece was the same wonderful colour right through. Near the steps hordes of ants would congregate, searching I suppose for crumbs. I used to pretend they were people, and felt a great satisfaction when the occasional adventurous citizen would venture along one of the long straight avenues between the tiles, which became, in my imagination, city blocks. He was turned back and returned to his fellows before he got very far, but I felt an anxious suspense at his brave exploration, and mentally ranked this loner as superior to the common, sheepherd mob nearer the edge of the verandah. (I am *sure* the garden was dried up; ants do not like damp ground.)

All I can remember of the dining room in which we children ate is that there was a cuckoo clock over the table — the same cuckoo clock which is now on the gallery of the big house, down near Uncle Stephen's table and the bucket that hangs from the roof to catch, or trace down, the leak he could never exactly locate. ("When it isn't raining, you don't know where it is," he explained, "and when it does rain, you can see where it is leaking, but you can't repair it.") So he hung a tin bucket below it, to catch the rain and to locate the leak. Why he didn't repair the thus identified spot I do not know. Perhaps it didn't happen when he was in a mood for carpentry.

I had never seen a cuckoo clock before, but I had seen pictures of them in my English story books, and I considered them "romantic." Later, when I graduated from my romantic period, my aesthetic soul rejected the crude, fake-peasant carving and gouging, the sticky-looking varnish and, eventually, the hoarse, rude, complaints of the little plaster bird who sprang out of the unlatched door each quarter hour, like one of my father's squawking hens who had just laid an egg. (An achievement so predictable, and so regular that I never could see why the biddies made such a fuss about it. It seemed to me both immodest and boring to be so boastful.)

I dimly remember a sitting room, but where it was, I cannot say. I can recall only one occasion when I was in it, to "borrow" a pen and ink for a drawing of Uncle Stephen's forget-me-nots which I had done for my father. The use of a pen was strictly forbidden, under Mother's general legislation governing Dangerous Instruments. Who knew when the sharp nib, doubly dangerous because infected with ink, might turn on the user and attack her? There was also the risk that I might (indeed, almost certainly would) stain my fingers, my costume, and even the table cover or floor. So this was a sneak visit, likely a fast one on that account, and my only recollection of the sitting room was that it was a lot of wicker furniture in it — quite likely the same furniture of which some is now down in the cellar of the Memorial Home. The only other room I remember was Granny's bedroom, which was, I think, at the same end of the house as Aunt Trix's and Uncle Stephen's, but in another wing. It led directly outside, so that Granny could get to her beloved outdoors and "garden" without having to go through the house.

From the front, or water side of the house, a winding path led down to the boat-house just before the point. The present, broader path is, essentially, the same one, though there was no such grandeur as the straight, cement-edged part that now leads to the wood and through the trellis Uncle Stephen built for Barbara's wedding. When I was at Orillia last October (1969), I was amazed to find that the end of the path, the part which goes past the site of the boat-house (it has been pulled down) still follows every curve and stretch that it did when I was little; my feet, like those of livery stable horse, needed no guide; they went where habit had taught them. Cottagers, like the Indians whose first paths traced the pattern of many Ontario roads, never thought of cutting down a tree, or razing a house to make way for a straight road; they went around the obstacles. Perhaps they lacked tools, or energy, but the end result was thoroughfares upon which one was in no danger of going to sleep, as one is on the traumatically monotonous throughways of today. On the Lakeshore Road at the south end of Lake Simcoe, for instance, there was, literally, history in each tree and boulder and shack. And so, Uncle Stephen's old path went where it had to.

I recall thinking that the winding path that went down to the boat-house was, like the cuckoo clock, "romantic," in the tradition of the *circa* 1900 *Girls Own Annuals* which I had inherited from one of the adults, because on either side of the path was a wide carpet of forget-me-nots. I remember, though, that my admiration was somewhat tempered by the frequent interference of mosquitoes, apparently ravenous for young flesh.

The boat-house, which was torn down and burned some years ago, stood just before the end of the point, on the inside shore of the bay. My uncle used the little loft over the boats as his study; I was told that *Sunshine Sketches* was written there. I do not think there was a study in the first house. (My brother, Stephen, says no, he remembers Uncle Stephen working in the boat-house.) I can just dimly remember going up into the loft, after he had his study in the new house, but it was rather musty, so I went back outdoors.

On the other side of the house, away from the lake, or at the back, was the lawn, with some flower beds near the verandah. This was where Stevie and Peggy Shaw, when they were older, used to play croquet. I think the grown-ups must have played there, too, because I remember the wickets and mallets, and half-heartedly trying to amuse myself by playing against an imaginary opponent. And I recall Uncle Stephen, who had been watching me, putting down his pipe on the table on the gallery, and putting his hand over mine to show me how to hold the mallet to get a better grip, and showing me how to put some force into my swing. I had the mallet with the blue stripes.

Visitors entered at the kitchen end of the house, just as they do now, but whether there was a fence about the place, and what its boundaries were, I cannot say. The "lawn," or untreed space on that side, was much larger than that at Granny's and it seems to me that there was a vegetable garden in view. But beyond that nothing that looked interesting enough to want to explore. All the interest was on the water side of the place.

This house, in what I guess was its final form, had an Italianate look to me. (I pored over whatever pictures of the Renaissance I could find, even before I was reading, and early fell in love with the plain, red-tiled houses, with their arcades and cloisters.) It came nearer to the look my uncle planned originally, it seems to me. My mother quotes him as saying, in a letter he wrote to her while on the Rhodes trip:

> When I build my house, I shall make it very plain but at the same time very large. I mean to plant a good avenue of trees leading up to it. In a few years with hard work it will begin to look fine. After it has been up two or three years, I shall brick

it with white brick and put in lattice windows in place of the
original ones and tile instead of shingles on the roof. Then, by
adding a sun dial, a nook and three wallflowers, it will become a charming English place.

While it never had the "good avenue of trees," unless one is to
count the short stretch of straight path going down to the lake, it
had the white look he obviously loved. Indeed, having less wood-
work outside than the present house, it looked much whiter.
Neither house got the lattice windows, but only this first house had
the tiles my uncle had planned for his dream home. It seems to me
that the present sundial, with the motto he inscribed himself in the
concrete base (*Brevas Horas – Longos Annos*) was in much the
same position in relation to the former house. The proportions of
the first house were very satisfying, aesthetically – no matter how
hodge-podge it may have sounded from Mother's description of its
construction. The total effect was of a large, long, quite low house,
with many long windows looking out over the water. The wallflowers must have been in the garden; Uncle Stephen would never
have dared show off his garden to Granny unless he had a wall-
flower for her to sniff. Yes, and there were primroses, too, so I
must have been there in very early summer one year.

The big grandfather clock at Uncle Stephen's house, and the
cuckoo clock did indeed, like the sundial, count out long years of
days whose hours, being filled with happiness, were short. My uncle
must have set himself very early in life the discipline so similar to
that which ruled my grandmother's days; it gave the lie to the
popular idea of a writer, as a temperamental soul who sits in his
ivory tower awaiting inspiration. Uncle Stephen never waited for a
mood; he sat down at his desk each morning long before anyone
else was up, and picked up his broad-nibbed fountain pen and
started to write – knowing that each page he finished, each hour
at that desk, broadened his practical education as a writer. Moods?
If a story he was telling, or an incident occurred, which spurred an
idea for an article, he scribbled down a note, or perhaps just tucked
it away in the great cranium. Simply to look at the scribbled note,

to recall a phrase or look was enough to put him back into the mood of the moment he wanted to record.

In the days I am speaking of, in the first house, and in the early years of the new house, my uncle worked in his study from five in the morning till ten. Perhaps he took a tea-break around our breakfast time, for I can remember him coming in and talking with us children, and later, too, when I was a teenager, his standing and asking about the day's plans. He didn't sit down and eat with us, so I suppose he had had something to eat earlier.

I recall that after his study was moved from the boat-house to the new house, that end of the verandah was forbidden territory while Uncle Stephen was working. I do not remember ever having been in it until last October.

Shortly after ten he went fishing or sailing. He wore an old fedora (so did my father, for that matter; none of us held with "dude" sports clothes). I think he must have worn a tie, even when he went fishing, for I can never remember him without one. All clothes were a matter of great interest to me, and men's clothes no less than women's. I used to put my father's gold cuff-links into his shirts for him, and watch, with fascination, the *legerdemain* with which he converted a slender strip of blue polka-dot silk into a neat neckpiece. However, although Uncle Stephen did consult my father on fishing, gardening and carpentry, he obviously never asked his advice on the art of making up a necktie.

Uncle Stephen's ties, although always present, gave one the impression of having first been thrown into a washing machine. They were tangled, rather than knotted; and they were generally bunched, rather than hung, to one side, revealing his top shirt button.

Again, no natty "sports shirts" for this sportsman; he wore an ordinary shirt, of the same type he would wear to lectures, I suppose. And a tweed trousers and waistcoat, no worse pressed than the one in which I saw him at our last meeting in Montreal. No worse . . . but no better. As Peter McArthur put it, in his introduction to a book on my uncle in the "Makers of Canadian Literature" series, "Allowing the eyes to travel downwards to his trousers, one has to admit they have a peculiar vagueness about the knees that can only be obtained by intensive scholarship."

I don't remember anything about the take-off for the fishing expedition except Uncle Stephen and several other males going down the path toward the boat house with fishing rods, and all sorts of pails and baskets.

In the sailing I was much more interested, as over at Granny's place Uncle Charlie often took us out in his skimming dish . . . a big, almost flat, open sailboat with broad decks. I never did anything more active than hold the tiller, with my uncle's hand over mine. But that was high action compared to sailing with Uncle Stephen. My memories of this boat are contradictory, for I recall it, lying alongside the dock at the boat-house as very long and sleek and pristine white . . . in fact the classic yacht one would expect of a famous and successful author. Strangely, though, the hold to which we children were consigned was small and stuffy, with no windows. I recall being hungry, too, and that when some sandwiches were passed down to us they were dry and stuck in my throat. Considering the incident now, I imagine that both impressions – that of the glorious vessel whose tiller I had confidently expected to take, and that of the cramped prison-ship in whose hold I found myself – were highly subjective. Bitterness and boredom may have detracted from the flavour of the sandwiches, too, just as it added to my jealousy of the adult crew above board, whose laughter came floating down to us in the hold. In fairness to Uncle Stephen, I imagine that he thought the children safer below decks, and likely thought we could make our own fun. Besides, he had liquid refreshment.

My uncle loved sailing from his earliest days, a passion which he inherited from his mother. In Granny's diary she often mentions sailing off the Isle of Wight with Peter Leacock and with other friends. And although, when she was on the farm, there could have been little opportunity when her children were small to get out on the water, she had a canoe when she was at Sutton, and quite often she would hobble down the steep steps in front of her house in Sutton so that Uncle Charlie could paddle her up the Black River.

I can recall little of the rest of the day's pattern at my uncle's house, other than going into Orillia with Aunt Trix, or swimming at the boat-house or over at their neighbour, Mrs. Shaw's place, on the other side of Old Brewery Bay. As for Uncle Stephen, I have practically no recollection of him after he went off to the boat-house in late morning, so I suppose perhaps he did not return until we children had had our tea and gone to bed.

This, I think, is as good a place as any to cut off, for a while, my early recollections of Uncle Stephen's house at Old Brewery Bay. In a later chapter, I will tell you a bit more about the present house, and about the people who lived in both of them.

My grandfather,
Walter Peter Leacock

Granny —
Agnes Emma Butler

Mother (Daisy Leacock Burrowes) and
my brother, William Stephen Leacock
Burrowes

Beatrix Hamilton, as "Jessica", before she married Uncle Stephen

Uncle Stephen with his son Stevie at Orillia

Uncle Stephen, Aunt Trix and little Stevie

Betty (Elizabeth Burrowes, later Kimball) age 3

Teddy, Charlie, Stephen, Dot, Carrie, Granny, Daisy, Jim, Maynell, Missie, Georgie

Bury Lodge, Granny's home in Sutton West, Ontario. Granny and Agnes Sheppard on verandah.

Betty, Dickie and Stephen Burrowes with two neighbours (standing)

Stevie (Stephen Lushington Leacock) at Old Brewery Bay

Granny, aged 80 or 85

The boathouse at Old Brewery Bay. Uncle Stephen wrote "Sunshine Sketches" in its loft

8

The Birthday Party in the Bush

PREAMBLE

My uncle very much liked to play God; or perhaps he was simply a thwarted playwright or stage director. Unite this predilection for making things happen with his enormous love for his family, intensified by his unfaltering conviction that few of them knew what was good for them, and it is only natural that we were frequently called upon to play puppets in schemes as splendid as his instincts.

I have often thought that this adult characteristic of my uncle's must have sprung from the terrible, hopeless years of his boyhood. The idealistic boy, sickeningly aware of the narrowness of his family's future, must have ached to set things right for his adored mother and his beloved brothers and sisters. When I first recall him he was already famous; and several of his brothers were also on the crest of success. Granny, after all the years of rented make-do's and lodging-house rooms, now had her own house and the cottage on the lake; she enjoyed, if not affluence, at least security and comfort. Except for Aunt Dot, all his sisters were married and happy. (And Dot herself was to marry later.) There was not a great deal he could do for his immediate family now. But the children, the little nieces and nephews – ah, that was another thing.

Body and bone of his dear mother, small, bright mirrors of his brothers and sisters and himself, the valiant, mischievous boys were second selves of Jim and Dick, of Charlie and George and Teddy;

the little golden-haired nieces must have reminded him of Missie and Carrie, of Dot and Maymee and Daisy. How he must have yearned to protect these defenceless little ones from all cruelty and want, to create for them a world wholly wonderful.

The reason why we were not given more frequent opportunities to enjoy Uncle Stephen's demonstrations of generosity was because such inspirations only came to him when we were *there*. And if he could not immediately get a scheme off the ground, he quickly lost interest. For this reason, mercifully for us, when we dispersed to our winter homes, we were left to muddle along without him. But summer was a different matter altogether.

One of his projects which I shall never forget was the birthday party in the bush.

THE BIRTHDAY PARTY

August 23 began with particular promise and shimmer. Granny's Lake was so calm and clear that, poised like young greenies on the cliff's rim before breakfast, we could see the crayfish scuttling over the blond-and-black striped sand bars. Nor could there have been a cloud in the sky, for my mother, scanning the heavens suspiciously for signs of peril, had pronounced, "Wear your hats, boys," and Stephen and Dickie had fetched the floppy white cotton mushrooms which they were compelled to wear on days of even pallid sunlight, Stephen's short stubble and even Dickie's thicker curls being deemed insufficient protection for the tender young brains within the shell-thin carapaces. Agnes and Margaret and I, thickly-maned as young ponies, were allowed to play bare-headed.

Plans for the day, of which I will tell you later, were already being lined out as, elbow to elbow at the oilcloth-covered table on the kitchen verandah, we speedily spooned up the hot porridge and gobbled down the thick, butter-sodden toast which was our breakfast no matter how hot the day.

At Old Brewery Bay, on the other side of the lake, the day ... the untouched basic day, as presented by nature for human embroidery or human tarnish ... must have begun on the same divine note. Waters as calm, skies as blue, the same pale-wine atmosphere, the same hush and promise of fulfilment of one's most extravagant dreams for summer.

On such a day it was natural that my uncle should have imagined himself God. And, equally predictably, for he was always responsive to Nature's moods, a kindly and generous God. Given, too, that this was little Stevie's birthday, it is no wonder that God should have aspired to a display of goodwill of Olympian dimensions.

I can imagine him beaming at his reflection in the mirror as he went about the morning rite of nicking himself with the razor. (Uncle Stephen, like all my Leacock uncles, was impatient of inanimate objects. It is difficult to believe that those superb intellects could not have mastered the mechanics of as simple an instrument as the straight razor, so I can only conclude that they so loathed the machine that they would not stoop to think through the necessary hold-razor-move-razor technique. At any rate, gouges, gashes and scars, white daubs of styptic pencil, often beaded with blood, and strips of sticking plaster, wrinkled (naturally), were as ordinary accessories of my Leacock uncles' get-ups as were ties and trousers.)

"I believe," I can hear Uncle Stephen thinking on that morning of mornings, beaming at his own reflection, "I believe I'll do something absolutely superb today." Then a pause as he resumes his nicking and gashing, spattering the bathroom walls with blood-specked lather as he clears the razor. "But what? And for whom?"

Nick. Nick. Pause. Sticking plaster. Go on, shave, think.

"Ah, I have it!" Whereupon he would emerge from the bathroom, eager to share his great idea, and to put it instantly into action.

He would start roaring for the housekeeper and she, as always braced for her role as God's second lieutenant, would hurry from the kitchen, where she was preparing breakfast.

"Tell Mr. Fred we'll be going to Sutton today," my uncle would announce.

Because, as we were soon to learn, the great treat that he had decided upon was to be a birthday party for dear Stevie, with all his dear cousins. At Sutton. And not only that – "I really am a terrific God!" he must have mused. "Who else would have thought of such an idea?" – the birthday party was to take place in Uncle Charlie's bush.

Whether my uncle had forgotten to make plans for Stevie's birthday, or whether, inspired by the grandness of the notion of a fête in the forest, he scrapped the idea of a party at home, I can only guess. Certain it is that, over on our side of the lake, the unwitting guests-to-be had had no warning of the benevolence in store for them until the moment Mother hailed us from the top of the bank, and we looked up to see Uncle Stephen's beaming face beneath the crumpled white Panama hat.

Even from this distance, about sixty feet, we could see his smile. "Betty! Margaret! Agnes! Stephen! Dickie! Boys! Come along! Stevie has a treat for you!" he called, the wooer's voice at its most honeyed, rich with loving-kindness.

The kindly Deity, looking down upon the cousins apparently aimlessly paddling about in the water, could not have realized that to leave the water on this day of days spelled an especial catastrophe. For the plans which had hastily formulated at breakfast were now well into their initial stages of execution. To Agnes and Margaret and I, conditions were ideal for playing mermaid, and at ten in the morning we were making preparations for an underwater garden party, on the lawns of the Mer-Queen's Palace. Extra seashell plates had been collected and prettily arranged on a large stone; menus had been decided upon, in which seaweed salad, rock cakes, and a gigantic sandcake with drift-wood candles were featured. Agnes and I were in serious conversation about our costumes; should we bind our tresses with ropes of pearls, or would coral look more summery? And Margaret was lecturing her mer-children regarding their manners for the event. (Margaret, who had at home an enormous family of dolls, had to do with imaginary babies for our underwater world.)

The boys, Christopher Columbus beating in each brave, ambitious breast, had launched the raft and struck out for the high seas the moment they got to the bottom steps. The high seas, I must in honesty report, were no higher than the tallest of the young mariner's cowlicks. The rule, as laid down by my mother, read "within your depth." The boys interpreted this to mean that as long as one hair on the head of the tallest of them remained dry, they were within the letter of the law. The presence among them that summer of one Cedric Smith was particularly fortuitous, since this gangly twelve-year-old, who was visiting us from Belleville, was a good head taller than my brother Stephen. By an even greater good fortune Cedric had a rather long head, sloping upward to a fine bristly cowlick, thus permitting the company to venture a good fifty feet further out on the sand bars than was normally legal.

I do not know exactly what the boys had planned for the day, since we females thought the boys' activities (building rafts, trapping each other below rafts, towing logs behind the raft, and perpetually redesigning and rebuilding the latest raft) pointless and boring. However, from the vigour of their cries, far out beyond our watery Fontainbleu, and from the speed with which they had pelted down the steps and pushed the craft off the rocks after breakfast, I imagine they were getting ready to set off on some particularly heroic voyage to a far-off shore. Who knows (anything was possible on a day like this) they may even have planned to journey to Mossington's Boathouse, at the mouth of the Black River, a project of which they had talked summer after summer, and even during the winter.

But now all this was to be changed. Silently, at our uncle's beck, the boys paddled and pushed the raft to shore and beached it on the rocks. Silently the girls forsook the shell dishes, the seaweed delicacies, the pearls and coronets of coral. Silently, heads down and shedding from our cotton bathing suits the last drops of our loved lake, we climbed the sun-baked spintered wooden steps to face our doom.

Silently, too, except for a nervous urging from mother, the adults awaited the victims. Uncle Stephen must have been impatient, as always, to get on with his plan, but the enjoyment of anticipation was apparently enough for the moment, and he did not speak until the first small, damp head appeared above the steps. Then he told us of the treat he had planned for us.

We changed into our clothes (khaki shorts and striped jerseys for the boys, khaki gym bloomers and middies for the girls) and gathered, a mute and mournful mob, beside the verandah. Then we were packed into cars. There were two of them – Uncle Stephen's big McLaughlin touring car, with Freddy Pellatt at the wheel, and Oswald King's Model-T. This latter vehicle was as bony and balky as the mare which Oswald apparently thought he was still driving. With his Adam's apple bobbing convulsively, he always grasped the wheel as if it were reins and urged the car on with stern "Giddaps" and soothing "Whoa, now girl!"

The kindly uncle supervised the loading process, unwittingly seating sworn enemies within pinching and glaring distance of each other on the jump seats. Finally all were stuffed in. Freddy and King revved up the motors. (Or did they crank them? I cannot recall whether this operation, which I certainly often witnessed, was an emergency measure at that date, or whether it was the normal way of starting a car.) Out through the hedge we chugged, and on along the noisy asphalt road to Uncle Charlie's bush, and the birthday party.

Even as emigrants gaze from steerage portholes for the last time upon the disappearing mother-shore, so did our young eyes, level with the edge of the car, strain from their sockets for a last look at the blue, abandoned lake. Goodbye to the mermaid's garden party. Goodbye to the odyssey to Mossington's. On toward endless exile in the bush; for, at our age, when time was measured between the first twitterings of the sand swallows and the sleepy murmur of the evening tide, a day could be eternal.

It is small wonder that Stevie, the small host in whose honour the celebration was being held, was not adored that day. We came as near to ignoring him as was politic, bearing in mind past punishments for dissension among cousins. I will record, to his credit, that he appeared embarrassed about it all, and was silent unless prodded by his father. "Overwhelmed by joy," was, I imagine, Uncle Stephen's interpretation of his son's taciturnity, and he therefore included him in the general priming up of enthusiasm. "Isn't this wonderful, Stevie?" he urged, turning around from his seat beside Freddy to where Stevie, wedged down between Cedric Smith, of the razor-sharp bones, and plump, perspiring David Ulrichsen, sat nervously smiling and trying to pretend he was one of the glamorous company of cousins. "Isn't it fun? All the cousins together on your birthday! We must do it again next year, mustn't we, dear?"

And "Yes, Dadda, let's do it next year," agreed the loyal little boy.

At the mention of future plans I recall a sensation in the pit of my stomach as if I had swallowed a splinter of ice. But neither I, nor any of the others, said a word. Any attempt to simulate enthusiasm was beyond us. Perhaps we were also too polite (or too politic) to express our true feelings. And we were afraid, too, that even the mildest assent would be wrongly construed.

I should perhaps mention at this point that never at any time did any of us understand the *reason* for Uncle Stephen's treats, any more than we understood how we had incurred many of our punishments. I was a grown woman, with children of my own, upon whom, they tell me, I inflicted equally incomprehensible unhappinesses, before I was able to perceive *why* we had been wrenched from our loved lake and put down among the flies and the heat and the boredom of Uncle Charlie's bush. It made no sense to me for a long time. What had we done to deserve it?

It was not the habit of the cousins to discuss, even among ourselves, our pains and pangs. Stoic little Britishers-by-remove, we endured but did not complain. Perhaps, if we had, we might have understood our elders better, and come to terms with them.

Lately, reading Uncle Stephen's story on Mother's Day, I have wondered how it was that he, who could so wittily describe how poor Mother suffered from her family's generous intentions, could never make the further connection, and bring the same insight to bear on his own role of Do-Gooder on such occasions as the birthday in the bush, the pilgrimage to the farm, my own marriage, etc. etc.

But let us now continue, along with the festive *entourage*, to the bush, which, as I have said, was on Uncle Charlie Leacock's farm. This most favourite uncle, Stephen's junior by two years and always very close to him, had bought the farm a few years before. I think he fancied himself as a gentleman farmer, but I can never remember anything growing on its acres except a few woody radishes, enormous raspberries guarded by gigantic, damp daddy-longlegs, and nettles and poison ivy. Plus the surrounding bush. To leave the cool, sparkling lake for this hot, humid, fly-infested forest, what was the point of it?

I cannot remember a great deal about the party itself. I have only a dim recollection of ploughing stolidly over rough hummocks covered with long damp grass, of legs being scratched by denuded raspberry canes, of arms, legs, neck and face being bitten by mosquitoes. (Uncle Charlie bred mosquitoes of even more monstrous scale than his berries and his spiders.)

At the picnic spot, where Mother and the aunts had spread a cloth and were arranging upon it paper plates heaped with sandwiches, a thermos jug filled with lemonade, and chimneys of paper cups, a host of flies awaited us. A large cake with thick white frosting was in the centre of the cloth, and the flies comparison-shopped between the rival gourmet treats of infant flesh and boiled icing. The cake had the advantage over us in that solicitous aunts kept shooing the flies away from it. No one bothered to protect us. We had been conveyed here to suffer.

The hot buzzing of the flies, and the whoosh of air as the women flailed and swatted at them, made the bush seem even hotter. As for the cake, it, like us, wilted in the heat, and the little wax candles drooped and ran into the sticky white icing, which had begun to sweat, and then to slide down off the sides of the cake. When, finally, the tapers were lit, their flame further increased the humidity of the bosk. When we finally forced ourselves to sing "Happy Birthday, Stevie," the chorus sounded more like a dirge than a paean of joy.

I recall all of us sitting about the picnic cloth, on prickly sticks and damp grass, unrelentingly silent, no matter how energetically Uncle Stephen encouraged us to enjoy ourselves, nor how pointedly our mothers tried to make us enter into the spirit of the celebration. I remember, too, feeling embarrassed for the grown-ups. Especially the mothers, who became increasingly brittle and gay as they sought to liven us up, and with a growing note of menace in their voices as they floundered against the unyielding wall of our silence. And even though he had been responsible, in a way, for the whole fiasco, I felt sorry for Stevie, who kept piping away like a small finch, "Isn't it grand, Dadda?" (Did he, perhaps, realize what a failure the affair was, yet feel compassion for his beloved Dadda?)

A lesser man than my uncle might have finally become discouraged. But God appeared totally unaware that we were not displaying our usual party behaviour. He beamed on, puffing at his pipe, and ceaselessly reminding us all of how happy we were.

Finally the miserable fête was finished, and the guests were released. We were deposited at the cottage, too late in the day, alas, to return to the lake. Uncle Stephen, still beaming, and with a tired little boy on his knee, waved goodbye to us from the big car, and set off for Old Brewery Bay. He never knew, I feel sure, that the Birthday Party in the Bush had been any less glorious a treat than he had planned it to be.

9

Pater Familias

I have described myself, in an earlier chapter, as an unwilling guest at Old Brewery Bay. Actually in my early childhood, it would be more accurate to term my state as a transplant. With no warning, let alone consulation concerning my wishes, I, like the other children from Granny's cottage who visited my uncle, would be abruptly wrenched from my natural terrain and set down again at Orillia. Invitations were in the form of a summons. "Don't you remember, he used to send for us?" my sister Margaret reminded me recently.

"He sent for us." Yes, I do remember. No warning letter, I am sure, or Mother would have prepared us for this disruption of our familiar routine. There was only the sudden jangling of the phone, more pre-emptory than the big bell at the Briars that summoned the hands in from the fields, or the appearance of the big car, with Uncle Stephen's driver, but without my uncle.

The phone or the envoy – and Mother's face at once taut and pleased. Pleased because the great man had singled out one of her offspring for his favour, tense because experience had taught her that the elected beneficiary was not always sensible of the honour being bestowed upon her or him.

Regarding these regal summons, I realize that the occasions actually followed a quite logical pattern. If you accept that the logic was Uncle Stephen's, not the guest's. Experiencing a sudden wave of warmth for his family, offspring-of-sibling category, my uncle must, of course, share the delicious sensation. "Come on in, everybody, the water's fine! Don't be afraid, little nieces and nephews, take Uncle Stephen's hand, come close to me!" That the chosen one might not, at the moment, share his emotion never occurred to him. And so, the summons by phone, or the driver dispatched to bring back one, or some of us, as though (from our point of view) we were a pair of rabbits from a pet shop, or a pailful of fishworms.

I should mention here, that my uncle's desire to see us did not always spring entirely from personal affection, but because he felt that his son, Stevie, should know his cousins. Neither do I think that was wholly from a sense of family duty, but was an attempt to surround his little son, an only child, with the sense of warmth and closeness that he and his brothers and sisters had enjoyed together. Family was such a big thing to him. Family. Home. Country. The first realities.

"He sent for us." Which would be chosen? Sometimes Uncle Stephen resolved this dilemma for my mother by specifying the victim. If Granny was going over on one of her periodic visits, a girl was generally chosen to act as lady-in-waiting, as it were. There were servants, of course, at my uncle's house, but the house was large and Granny's room away at one end, and my uncle must make sure that his mother, most-honoured guest, must not want for anything while she was within his walls.

Sometimes, however, my uncle apparently would just invite "one" or "some" of the children. Then, when the invitation was relayed, a great quarrel would ensue – not, as you will now have guessed, for the privilege of going to Old Brewery Bay, but to avoid having to go. Then my mother must not only break up the battle, but make the decision, comfort the loser – and worry for fear the host might twig to the guest's unwillingness.

"He sent for us." Yes, I remember, that is the way it was. The abrupt summons, the sudden uprooting, the swift set-down. Granny's cottage and the whole known world (Belleville, by midsummer seemed so far away it scarcely counted) blacked-out. In its place a raw new scene, and strange new people who seemed not to notice the oddness of one's advent. An acreage whose edges were forbidden, not by avuncular admonition, but by fear of the unknown. A house in no room of which I knew one corner, one space of floor, one stick of furniture. Ceilings so high I nearly toppled when I looked up. Plaster walls as in a city house instead of worn board or rounded bark, as at Granny's dear cottage. I dared not go through a door because I knew not what was on the other side of it. I remember standing in the middle of Aunt Trix's bedroom, not knowing what to do or even who she was. (She asked me if I would like to have a sleep, and I thought this very strange, for surely she must see that a big girl of my age was far beyond afternoon sleep.)

Even outdoors it was no better.

Urgency and a sense of apprehension in Scene I; a trance-like quality to Scene II. No comfortable bridge between, no mutual waters. I cannot even remember the trip to Orillia. Quite likely, I was in the back seat of my uncle's car, and so low and far back that I didn't see anything of the road.

I cannot remember the seeing-off, I cannot remember the welcome. Just an unexplained dislocation of my life, the feeling of time stopping, of living by a clock that might never tick again. For how was I to know that I would ever again see Sutton?

My first memory of my cousin Stephen, Uncle Stephen's only child, was in his first house, in his own nursery. He could have been only about two or three, because he was wearing a little tan-coloured cotton romper affair. He was already committed to glasses, as I recall, which, large and dark-rimmed, as children's glasses always were then, made him look like a small owl. But even though he could not possibly have been old enough to read, the room had long bookcases along the walls, and there were many books. I went for them like a homing pigeon, for like most half-intelligent children I had taught myself to read long before I went to school. (It hurts, to admit this, but this fact is not really so impressive when you learn that I was nearly seven before I started to school. One of the direct influences Uncle Stephen had upon us as children was that he then had a theory that a child's eyes were not yet equal to the strain of a continuous day of study. To my mother's built-in reverence for her big brother's opinions on all matters academic was added the further argument of convenience. We lived a mile away from the nearest school in Belleville, a long walk for young legs, and a bitter one in winter. So we were kept at home till we were seven.) Whether I read Stevie's books, or whether I simply looked at the pictures and made up my own stories, I cannot remember, but I do recall that Stevie and I spent a lot of time together in the pleasant room with the books and the toys, and the lake and the sunlight outside. I do not recall his paying any attention to me, he would sit quietly on the floor at his side of the nursery, while I sat on mine, close to the book-shelves. We were both quite content in our own way.

The only discordant note in my relationship with him was that Stevie had a very beautiful big rocking horse. It had brown glass eyes with the same fiery expression I had observed in the eyes of Uncle George's Lavender, a very nervous and spirited little mare. This steed of Stevie's also had a pelt of smooth brown fur. "Real fur," I thought, though maybe it was not. And the harness was shiny and new. I had always wanted a rocking horse, ever since I had seen one in B. A. P. Roberts Toy Shop in Toronto, when I was three. I had never had one, not only because it was a very expensive toy even for parents whom Santa helped out so generously, but because, I suppose, Mother did not believe a quiet little girl who rarely played with anything except her dolls and her crayons could really want a rocking horse.

I wanted most terribly to mount Stevie's hunter. (Of course it had to be a hunter – I knew nothing of race horses at this point.) But I felt I was too old; that I would lose dignity by such an action. On the other hand, Stevie was obviously too little to ride it, and appeared unaware of the animal. I used to look often at its beautiful liquid eyes, its prancing hooves, its glossy black mane and tail. It became almost alive to me, and it seemed to me that it was pleading to go for a canter. But each day it became more and more impossible for a grown young lady like myself to play with a rocking horse. And so we sat, I with the books, Stevie with his teddybear, and the princely equine prancing and rearing but forever denied the green fields and fences for which his noble heart longed.

In my early visits, when the first house was still in existence, my memories of Aunt Trix are sharper than those of my uncle. I recall her walking along the path toward the boat-house with her big black German shepherd, and showing Mother the flowers on the floor of the red-tiled gallery at the back of the house; asking my father, of whom both she and Uncle Stephen were very fond, about his garden, talking to him in a low voice; talking to one of the maids in the children's dining room; looking at a picture I had drawn; taking Stevie's hand and helping him walk. I remember a slight argument with her on this question of my "afternoon sleep." In our family, only my baby sister had an afternoon sleep, and I said "No, thank you!" but Aunt Trix insisted I lie down on her big bed. I remember I couldn't sleep, and resentfully watched the sunlight through the curtains, and felt a little annoyed with Stevie, who was, I felt, indirectly responsible for my enforced idleness, because he had a nap each afternoon.

Aunt Beatrix seemed very tall to me, perhaps because my mother and my "real" aunts were small (most of them five-foot-two or under). She wore dresses that looked strange to me. I remember a long tunic-like dress of linen, grey or some other neutral shade, with short sleeves and a squarish neck. Her clothes were quite different from those worn by my very elegant Aunt Ethel (Uncle George's first wife), and my rather dashing little bachelor Aunt Dot, and by Aunt Gypsy from Calgary; or even from the simple summer cottons Mother and Aunt Carrie wore at Granny's cottage. Aunt Trix's clothes were very plain without having any great style or sophistication to them, but they looked as if they could only belong to her. Her heavy, dark hair was piled on top of her head.

My aunt had a lovely deep voice, with a great deal of colour in it and, like Uncle Stephen, she always listened intently when she was talking with you, as if she really cared what you said. There was never any "talking down" to children with either of them. I liked her quietness. (Whatever I may have said about our general unwillingness to leave Sutton for Orillia, we were still very fond of Uncle Stephen and Aunt Trix.) And I recall Aunt Trix's calmness and gravity as a cool pool after the hurly-burly waters of life with the rest of our adults.

Ralph Curry, in his biography of my uncle, has remarked on Aunt Trix's vivacity and her "almost electric beauty." Beautiful she was, according to my mother, and to the photo my mother had on her dresser of Beatrix as a girl, which must have been taken about the time she married Uncle Stephen. It shows long, dark hair over her shoulders and deep, soulful eyes. But even in the photo, her smile was quiet; and I recall her as very grave ("sad" I thought, as a child, perhaps not understanding gravity, being accustomed to vivacious women) and serious. That, too, is the impression I had of her from my mother — of a woman of very deep emotions and steadfast character. I recall my mother telling me of dinner parties at Côte des Neiges and (whether these were from my mother's first hand experience or from Trix's letters or summer conversations I do not know), and although I knew they entertained a lot, in their own house, I had the impression that my aunt was sometimes shy and rather over-powered by the "smart set" which was lionizing my uncle. Mother said Uncle Stephen teasingly remarked about "Little One" sitting silently through these affairs. There were tales, too, of my uncle's occasional philanderings and Trix's unhappiness. Perhaps the "electric Trix" belonged to the early days; or maybe the sadness which impressed me was only the last time I saw her, which was, I think, the summer before she died of cancer.

Of that terrible event, I vividly recall my mother's accounts of my uncle's incredulous grief, his rage at anyone who suggested that Trix's case was hopeless, and at my mother, who begged him to try Christian Science. My mother told me later that Beatrix pleaded with him to let her die at home, but Uncle Stephen, furious with her for accepting the idea of death, hurried her across the Atlantic to Liverpool, where what was called the "lead treatment" promised hope for cancer cases.

The clinic was filled to overflowing, and my gentle aunt died, ten days before Christmas, in a small, windowless room. My cousin Stevie, then ten, says he remembers the nurse coming into their hotel room and Uncle Stephen saying, "Is it over, then?" and the nurse saying "It's not long now, Mr. Leacock," or something to that effect.

I think my own early memories of them both, no matter what my impression of Aunt Trix, must belong to the days when they were happiest. They had the house they loved, and summer by the lake; if they were worried over Stevie's slow growth (later a matter of quite terrible concern to my uncle), it was not yet the almost-confirmed fear. Granny and my uncles and aunts, Trix's mother, and all sorts of relations and connections and friends were constantly coming and going; Uncle Stephen had his writing, his fishing and sailing; they both loved the garden. It was, as I recall, a happy house. I have no backplay of angry voices there, nor, as later, of fearful scurrying to avoid my uncle's not-infrequent rages.

Like most children, I suppose, I was sensitive to "atmosphere," to tension among people, to their moods. And I recall my uncle's house as having an harmonious atmosphere. I do not recall any great rollicking or boisterous langhter, but I do remember my uncle's chuckle, the many happy voices. I think back to his talking with my father, that time Daddy took me to Orillia. I remember Uncle Stephen asking my father's advice about the garden (although my father was a wonderful gardener, as my mother remarked, so was Uncle Stephen). I think his getting Dad to talk about the garden was just Uncle Stephen's way of "putting the ball into his court," so to speak, of making the other person feel as if he really cared for their opinion. I cannot remember exactly what was said all that long time ago, but I do remember his asking Dad very specific questions . . . just how far apart should the rows of peas be – or something of that nature. They were very deep in conversation about it, and they got up and walked out into the vegetable garden so that my father could give him a practical demonstration. They talked about fishing, too, which was with my father, as with Uncle Stephen, almost a religion rather than a sport.

I do not remember a great deal of laughter between my father and my uncle. My father was a fairly serious man, and of course the subjects they were discussing (gardening and fishing) were serious subjects. But, again, the harmony of two low, pleasant voices. (For my mother, I imagine, it would have been inconceivable to marry a man with a strident or in any way unpleasant voice.)

There is only one incident of any importance in which my Uncle Stephen figured that I can definitely place in this early, first-house era. He came into the nursery one morning – not a usual occurrence, since while we were having breakfast he was still writing, and later, around ten o'clock, he usually went fishing or sailing. I believe at that time he was still using the upstairs room in the boathouse as a study, so it is quite likely that he did not, always, come back up to the house before he went out on the lake. So this was likely just before lunch, or after Stevie's afternoon sleep. I was sitting on the floor drawing, and felt someone watching me. I looked up to see Uncle Stephen. I remember we talked about my picture, how I got this or that effect, and why the horse was standing up on his hind legs. (He wasn't; he was jumping a fence, but I hadn't put the fence in yet.) Like Uncle Charlie, Uncle Stephen discussed the matter with me as if we were the same age, and as if I knew more about painting than he did. (For that matter, I likely did. As Stevie reminded me lately, his father wasn't in the least interested in painting, nor in music; his voice was his instrument.)

After we had finished discussing the picture, he leaned down and he picked Stevie up, and I went back to my crayons. I don't remember him tickling Stevie, or making a great fuss about him, just his holding him and looking at him, and the quiet and loving sound of his voice. Again, as I have already remarked, and will likely do so again, my uncle's voice was the thing which really meant "Uncle Stephen" to me. And never was it more beautiful . . . more loving, more sweet, and later, when he first began to fear that Stevie might never be robust, more filled with pain . . . than when he addressed his little son.

As I mentioned in an earlier chapter, we children eventually came to realize, through attracting a measure of publicity not extended to our playmates, that Uncle Stephen was famous beyond our hedge. Aside from the burden of notoriety, there were other disadvantages to having a famous uncle. For my part, as an aspiring author I found it very discouraging to have my genius credited to heredity. ("She can't help it; Stephen Leacock is her uncle," as one teacher put it.) I felt that, having had his day, he might have moved over and made room for fresh talent – changed his name, or paid more attention to his teaching, for instance. When he continued to monopolize the stage, I had no choice but to abandon my literary career.

Still, not only was he famous, according to my playmates he was rich. While I still resented his interference in my career, I could see that there might be advantages to having an uncle who belonged to the power *élite*. I looked forward to rubbing shoulders with High Society, as typified by a group of young men and women, resplendent in evening dress and seated in a theatre box, whom the cartoonist, Fish, depicted in the frontispiece of one of Uncle Stephen's books. Indeed, for a long time I thought Fish had sketched the group at one of my uncle's *soirées*. Bare-back evening dresses, ropes of pearls, liveried servitors and cocktail shakers were the least I expected of my uncle's domestic scene.

What a come-down was the reality of Old Brewery Bay! I have described how simply Aunt Trix dressed (not so much as an osprey plume for her hair, let alone a bare back); not a cocktail shaker to be seen, let alone heard; and, if anything, many of the people who came and went at my uncle's house appeared to be low, rather than high society.

However, in one respect, my uncle did, in a way, live up to my expectations. His domestic staff, by and large, did seem worthy of a famous author. Over at our side of the lake, there was Granny's housekeeper, Lang, but if she wore a uniform it must have been of the summer cotton variety, whereas the two maids Uncle Stephen brought with him from the house on Côte des Neiges Road wore crisp white aprons over black cotton uniforms. Moreover, they spoke French, acknowledged tongue of High Society. This was right in the "Did you ring, Madam?" tradition of a play I had been taken to at the Royal Alex when I was six, and pictures on the back of *Punch* advertising Abdullah cigarettes. They supplied an exotic contrast to old Lang, and the little summer "hired girls" at the cottage, who were almost as familiar with us as our cousins, and the cosy Indian women who used to do the washing and ironing for us when we were at the Grange.

But the rest of Uncle Stephen's staff was an awful let-down. Jones, the gardener whom, as my uncle said, he had taken out of the army and put at the other end of a hoe, ordered the boys and Stevie about in a manner rather less respectful than our parents. (Now I realize, it was with good cause; he knew all the vices boys are prone to, such as gravel-flinging, chasing the horse, teasing the St. Bernard, playing Indians in the corn and eating green apples; the knowledge did not tend to promote respect.) "My," I remarked recently to Stevie, "Jones was a fierce-looking man." "No, I wouldn't say that," my cousin replied, and I though he looked a bit nonplussed. A bit later, I realized that my impressions were likely coloured by my brothers' awe of the gardener, whereas Stevie, being neither as wicked as my brothers, and having long outgrown what vices he may have shared with them when little, had also outgrown what fears he may once have had of Jones. In addition to Jones, my uncle had always several family retainers. Literally.

These retainers – many of whose period of retention by my uncle was very short – were actually drawn from the ranks of his family. Nieces, nephews, cousins, in-laws. They worked in the secretarial or clerical departments, at either or both houses, the educational, or in the social services.

Barbara Nimmo, my Aunt Carrie Ulrichsen's older daughter, became my uncle's "lady of the house" and his secretary after Aunt Beatrix died. In the latter capacity she followed my sister, who had been "sent for," in the imperial manner, to take over my uncle's secretarial duties. Margaret resigned after only a few weeks; the typing was easy enough for her, but my uncle's lightning-swift changes of mood were more than she could take. Barbara, older, and with the blood of her phlegmatic Norse father in her veins, succeeded where Margaret failed.

My cousin Douglas was commandeered to give young Stevie swimming lessons. Freddy Pellatt, Aunt Trix's young uncle, drove the car for a time. Visiting nieces and nephews did part-time stints as harvesters of vegetables and tenders of poultry. I do not know whether my sister was actually engaged in the administrative end of this particular field, or whether she was in the purchasing department for the project, but she recounted, one summer after she returned from Orillia, my uncle's latest experiment in practical economics. Turkey raising was his current enthusiasm. Discovering that what he considered an undue amount of time was being spent in keeping the turkey pens clean, he had linoleum cut to fit the pens. Cut, but not tacked down. No, each day the pieces of linoleum were withdrawn from the pens, laid outside and hosed down, allowed to dry in the sun, then laid on the floors again. Familiar with other accounts of my uncle's home economics, I am reasonably sure that he did not figure in the cost of the linoleum, nor of the washers-down when he toted up the profit per bird of the turkey-raising venture. As I recall, the exquisite boudoir was in vain, for the turkeys were stricken with some strange malady, and dropped dead, one after another, before they reached dinner-plate size.

But all in all, by its very magnitude, and by the utter "class" provided by the two French maids, the staff at Old Brewery Bay was quite a cut above Granny's comparatively rustic helpers, and our own modest arrangements at Belleville. (We had only one resident maid, and an old Indian "washerwoman." Granted, the latter was a granddaughter of Joseph Brant, but she came in only once a week, which made a total staff of one and one-seventh.) So when I was discussing my rich uncle with my peers I spread his staff as thickly as possible. There was no need to mention the fact that Aunt Trix didn't wear pearls and that Uncle Stephen had only a McLaughlin instead of a Cadillac. No matter what my personal doubts might be about Uncle Stephen's foothold in High Society, at least I could put a good face on things when I was back with my schoolmates in Belleville. How many of them had rich and famous uncles with maids who spoke French, and special servants for the turkeys?

10

...and Genial Host

"It will be a big house, with room for you all,' Stephen said to me the day he bought the land." So my mother wrote, speaking of the time she witnessed the signing of the deed to Old Brewery Bay.

She witnessed the deed of purchase ... and she and many hundreds of guests in the forthcoming years could testify to the fact that my uncle did indeed build a house that had "room for you all." He only meant the family then, his mother and brothers and sisters. But Old Brewery Bay, although its rooms were only nineteen in number, seemed capable of containing any number of guests ... the husbands and wives of his brothers and sisters, the nieces and nephews, hosts and armies of friends. It seemed indeed big enough to house the whole world. His great, hospitable spirit made it so.

As I have already explained, the house did have certain physical imperfections which might tend to temper one's enjoyment of a visit there. Torture-rack beds, punch-hole window screens, and taps from which no water ran might easily discourage the novice guest. He might rise from a sleep whose hours had been decimated by the attentions of Brewery Bay's particularly vicious brand of mosquitoes, and totter to the basin to slap himself awake with cold water. He would turn on the tap – only to find no cold water. No water at all, in fact. A deep brown stain on the bone-dry enamel would mutely testify that water had run in the past. But not now. Not for him. Nerve-ridden, insect-harried, unshaven, unlaved, he would go down to breakfast.

There he would be met by his host, beaming with bonhomie. "How did you sleep?" my uncle would inquire. Then, without waiting for an answer, "Wonderful! Wonderful! Nothing like it, is there?" And the guest could agree with fervour. There could, truly, be nothing like Old Brewery Bay's guest accommodations anywhere – except today, in a $9-a-night room in Paris at the height of the tourist season. But soon, sitting at breakfast, and swept along on the great tide of *joie de vivre* that welled from his host like the waters of a spring-fed lake, the guest would forget his aching bones, his insect bites, his bristling beard. He would begin to see Old Brewery Bay through my uncle's eyes. At the week's end, off he would go to tell his friends about this miraculous house, so perfect in every detail, and, yes, a big house, big enough for all.

When I was small, although I remember a continual coming and going of people and cars, I do not remember much about the people outside the family. I know quite a few famous writers stayed there from time to time, but if they were there when I was they were just a part of a conglomerate of foreign grown-ups, and of no great interest to me. Aside from Granny, Uncle Charlie and my brothers, my sister and my cousins, and perhaps Aubrey Morphy and Aunt Trix's mother, Mrs. Hamilton, I cannot recall any other house guests until I was there years later, in my teens.

As I have said my grandmother was a frequent and honoured guest in my uncle's house. And, as soon as she arrived, either Agnes or Margaret or myself would be summoned, to assume our duties as ladies-in-waiting. "Do you remember," my sister said to me recently, "we used to go over to brush Granny's hair?" And the years rolled back, and I was again standing beside my granny, with her ivory brush in my hand, and with the silvery locks, finer than the finest silk, fanning out into an aura about her face. We used to fight for the privilege of brushing Granny's hair, Agnes and Margaret and I. So she would take one of us along to Orillia, to brush her hair, and carry her folding chair out to the lawn, set up her water-colours for her, and change her paint-water when it got dirty. (On the wall in the office of the Stephen Leacock Memorial Home I saw hanging a little water-colour Granny had done of the house from outside her room. Like me, she must have preferred the red tile roof of the first house; she made the roof vermilion, though it was actually grey shingle.) We would run other small errands for her too – messages to my uncle, letters to be taken to the driver for his next trip to the post office. And above all, one was expected to stay close to her, because she often had what she termed "giddy spells," and her children watched over her zealously.

I don't believe Uncle Stephen was ever happier than when he could play host to his adored mother. He had found many ways of showing his concern and love for the woman whom he, when little more than a boy, had rescued from the tyranny of his father. Certainly it must have made him happy when he visited her at her house in Sutton, where she was now comfortable and at peace after the many hard years of her early and middle age. Nevertheless, it must have been best of all to have her close to him, in the house which, as my mother says, "he had built through his own hard work."

Tina, the housekeeper who was with him for so many years, recollected, when I talked with her a little while ago, how he used to sit on the edge of Granny's bed while she had her early cup of tea. "They were always laughing together," Tina reminisced, "and both so happy." And Tina added the corollary which was natural to almost everyone whenever they spoke of my grandmother: "She was such a wonderful woman."

Quite aside from filial regard and love, Uncle Stephen was very close to his mother intellectually. Agnes Emma Butler had been a well-educated young woman before she married Peter Leacock. She tells, in her journal, of her clergyman father teaching her Latin when she was ten years old, so that she could take classes with her cousin Tom, with whose family she was sent to live because of her own father's failing health. My uncle has written, in *The Boy I Left Behind Me*, of her attempts to educate her sons herself. But, as he said, "It was no use, we knew it was only Mother." Still, she had learned her arithmetic and history, in an age when an academic education was not considered necessary to young females, even those who had the leisure to spend on it.

Granny took an active interest in politics, and read contemporary writers avidly. (She already had the "greats" of the past at her fingertips.) I recall reading Galsworthy, Michael Arlen, and F. Scott Fitzgerald from her shelves, and many other authors who were popular at the time. It seems to me that both on Uncle Stephen's visits to Sutton, and when she was staying at Old Brewery Bay, the main subjects of their long discussions were literature and history. He listened with apparent respect to her opinions, especially about his own writing. About the only time when I can remember any feeling of friction between them, in fact, was that one occasion when she took him to task about what she considered a deterioration in the quality of his writing. Some time later my mother told me how concerned Granny had been about his "churning out" so much writing, and that she was fearful his gifts might be waning.

I think this must have been about 1930, for I know my mother at least attributed the feverish pace at which he was producing as due to the fact that he had lost money (about $40,000 I heard) on the stock market, and was fearful that he might leave his son in want. How much my mother romanticized and embroidered here, and how much was fact, I don't suppose anyone knows for sure. My cousin Stevie says his father never needed to have had any real concern about stock market losses, as almost all his investments were very solid, long-term stocks and bonds, and were unaffected by even the great crash. However, I recall Uncle George saying he had lost money, and if it was $40,000 that would be enough to worry about at that day's dollar value. (I have read that $40,000 was his peak earnings per annum for his writing.)

Uncle Charlie, my beloved bachelor uncle from Sutton, used to spend fairly long visits with Uncle Stephen. One time he escorted my brothers part of the way to Orillia. I think he went up to Toronto, and to meet the train from Belleville. Both my brothers, who were very small at the time, still remember his making a big fuss because Dickie had taken off his tie. Uncle Charlie's ties were, in general, only slightly less casual than Uncle Stephen's . . . still, crooked and rumpled though it might be, a tie was *de rigeur*, even in summer. And they recall being taken fishing in a big old motor boat.

Young Stephen was very fond of our uncle Charlie, and Tina recalled the many times when, on the spur of the moment, they would put together a picnic and go over to see Uncle Charlie in his "bush" at Sutton; this was, apparently, even after Stevie was out of his teens.

Stevie told me, too, of Uncle Charlie's coming to pick him up once at Casa Loma, where he had been visiting with his uncle, Sir Henry Pellatt. When the butler announced Uncle Charlie's arrival the family was still at table. "Tell him to wait in the hall," replied Sir Henry, whose wealth apparently exceeded his polish. My cousin told me he felt very embarrassed and indignant for Uncle Charlie, but that the latter thought it was a great joke.

The constant arrival and departure of cars at Uncle Stephen's gave me a pleasant feeling of being part of a rather more wordly scene than we were accustomed to in Belleville. (My father was not only too poor to drive a car. He didn't "believe in them" as the family expression was. Not "believe" in the sense of belief, say, in flying saucers, or whatever their equivalent was in those days, but in the same way that Mother didn't "believe" in drink.) My father liked walking, and he generally walked on the road . . . safe enough in the outer regions of Belleville when we were little, but decidedly unsafe as these suburbs became the busy centre of the city. "It's getting so a man can't even walk down the street," my father used to sigh, as he gave way to a pre-emptory honk and moved over to the side of, not the sidewalk, but the road.

Aunt Trix drove in and out of Orillia almost daily, I suppose to shop; Fitz Shaw's car stood for hours in Uncle Stephen's drive, gravel flew announcing one of Uncle George's impulsive appearances; Aunt Dot's little roadster was generally there at least once a summer and visitors from Montreal arrived almost every weekend. The MacLaughlin was always on the go, too, taxiing weekend guests from and to the train.

As I say, I never took part in any of the summer dinner parties or grown-up activities. The only time I was at Orillia when I was old enough to have done so (I was at high school, and some summer-job friends dropped me off on their way on up the lake), it was late Friday night, after dinner, and Barbara and several of her friends were already on their way out. I cannot remember what we did on Saturday night.

True to family tradition, I had not given my uncle warning that I was coming. "In Out of the Storm," he announced dramatically looking down at me.

Mary Harvie (my Uncle George's widow, now married again) has given me, however, a very good picture of their weekend visits to Uncle Stephen's place. "The first thing Stephen said to us was always, 'Will you have a drink?'" she recalled. "As he said to George, 'You don't know, they may have been on the road for hours, and are dying of thirst.'" Even though she and Uncle George were family and he was on vacation, Mary said Uncle Stephen always made an event of the Saturday night dinner party. The drinks would be served in the big sitting room with the red curtains, and with them sardines or salmon, or some similar dainty as *hors d'oeuvre*.

Dinner was then served on the long gallery, with fresh-cut flowers on the table ("I always had to do the flowers," reminisced Tina) and place cards, each with an amusing comment or verse beside the name. I have heard so much about these amusing place-cards, and invitations in verse, both for Old Brewery Bay dinner parties and for more formal occasions at Côte des Neiges Road, but no one can ever remember enough to quote. I dimly recall Mother reciting a verse from an invitation, in which Fitz and her two sisters were referred to as the "Three Graces from the Fair Isle," or some similar conceit. (Mrs. Shaw came, I believe, from Prince Edward Island.)

The *pièce de rèsistance* was often soup made from the fresh pods of young peas, Mary told me and Uncle Stephen would pause, with his spoon at his lips, and say, "Isn't this delicious? Isn't it superb? Fresh peas, picked from the garden!" Young broilers, also from the estate, were often the main course. Or trout which had been caught in his own stream. Tina says he was continually reminding

93

dinner guests that "everything was on the house," a play on the phrase which appeared always to delight him. He would go to a vast amount of paperwork to prove how *little* per plate it cost him to feed a summer's total of guests, which equalled a small army. In his role of Professor of Economy, he of course disposed of such incidentals as labour, poultry-feed and garden-seed as "practically nothing" and would not even enter them in the account.

Uncle Stephen's pride in his "home-grown" table was typical of him. I have heard so many people remark that his delight in his own achievements was one of his most endearing qualities. It didn't come across as vain or boasting, because he was just as pleased with other people's success.

Mary Leacock told me of one dinner party which was not "on the house," at least, in the literal sense. It seems that early one evening, as they were enjoying their hors d'oeuvres and before-dinner drinks, Uncle Stephen began to lament the fine sailing wind they were missing. Someone remarked it was a shame they couldn't have dinner on the boat.

"And why not?" retorted the host. "Come, George, give me a hand"; and in short order the men were carrying the table, cloth, plates, wine glasses, cutlery, flower centre-piece, food, and all to the dock. Tina apparently took over then, and packed the edibles into hampers and boxes. So this dinner party was "on board" rather than "on the house."

I do not know how that dinner party ended, but as a general rule, after coffee had been served, the host of Old Brewery Bay would say goodnight to his guests. Ten o'clock was his bedtime, summer as well as winter.

As always, he was up long before the guests the next morning with several hours of writing behind him by the time they came down for breakfast. Then he would bring what he had written, and read it to them, again stopping to laugh. "Oh dear, George, this *is* good, isn't it?" he would say. "Isn't that funny? It's really very funny!"

It may well be that Uncle George might be the best possible critic of how good it was; very often Uncle Stephen's stories were borrowed from Uncle George. If anything, Uncle George had a quicker appreciation of the humour in everyday situations ("situation comedy") than the famous writer. I can never remember being with him, and I was often with him, that he did not have something funny to tell me, something that had happened as he came in, during his last business trip, in the kitchen, or at the Hunt Club or the track. None of my uncles ever had any need of "store jokes," the kind of stock stories after-dinner speakers generally relate again and again.

Even in bereavement, Uncle George could see the humorous side of a situation. I remember his telling me, for example, about having just visited an undertaker to arrange for the burial of a dear friend. He asked, in a perfunctory way, I suppose, about the undertaker's children. "Freddy (or whatever) must be getting to be a big boy, now," suggested Uncle George. The undertaker glowed with pride. "That he is, Mr. Leacock," he replied, "and such a help, you wouldn't believe. Why he can set in them tacks just as straight as you could." The tacks to which he referred were the upholstery tacks for the coffin lining. Uncle George mimicked the undertaker's proud tones exactly, and set me laughing even though I knew how badly he felt about his friend's death.

Even when the story was Uncle Stephen's own, he would go over it with George, between the two of them refining and perfecting it until Uncle Stephen was satisfied with it. And all the time they would be laughing heartily at their own jokes.

My mother wrote of her brother's delight in *Sunshine Sketches*. She said, "I was staying with him at Orillia in September 1912, when his copies of the book came from the publishers ... he read the opening chapters aloud ... he stopped often to call my attention to some passage he felt very pleased with. He loved a joke ... his own or anyone else's, and I think he got more pleasure out of *Sunshine Sketches* than anything else he wrote."

Critics of my uncle's writings have remarked that Stephen Leacock's humour is "talk" humour. He writes as if he were talking, and you will find his stories five times as amusing if you read them aloud to someone else.

I did not discover this fact till late . . . in fact after my children had been going to school several years. They had been studying Stephen Leacock (studying not reading, it must have been) at school. "Was Uncle Stephen really funny Mother?" my son Stephen asked me. I started to say, "I never thought so" (when I first tried reading him I was too young to appreciate his humour, and I was so often made to read from *Sunshine Sketches* at school that I become fed up with his works), but I thought I had better let the boys judge for themselves. So I had Stevie bring me *Laugh with Leacock*, and started to read "My Financial Career" aloud. You can guess the rest. Before I was half way down the first page, I was laughing so hard I could not go on. That was the first time I realized that my uncle *spoke* his stories first, then wrote them. Or if he did not actually do this, he mentally told the story to a live audience as he wrote it.

I should mention that besides the hundreds of guests at Uncle Stephen's table, and in his beds, each summer, there were many others who enjoyed fringe hospitality. A typical instance of this company was a sailing acquaintance of mine, Fred McKenzie, of Toronto, who apparently knew my cousin Irving Sheppard when they were boys. They camped on Uncle Stephen's farm one summer, and Fred recalls that Uncle Stephen used to have a man carry them a pail of fresh milk each morning, knowing that the stalwart woodsmen would not go all the way into town to carry milk to supplement their camper's diet of beans and fish.

My brother Dick lent me a journal which my uncle kept the last summer he was at Old Brewery Bay. It is titled, in scratchy inked handlettering on the cover, HOUSE, GARDEN & FISH BOOK VOL. 2 1943. This was the summer before Uncle Stephen died, and that he enjoyed that summer fully is evident from the entries.

In spite of the title, the journal is little concerned with the house, although he methodically recorded the coming and going of guests. "Tu. June 1, 1943," the first entry starts off, "Stevie, Henry Janes left for Toronto, driving . . . June 2 Fitz left afternoon train for Montreal . . . " and, after noting some sixty-four arrivals and departures of guests and family (he recorded only the weekends and the odd weekday), the vehicles by which they travelled, the hours at which they came and went, he closed with the final entry, on October 11: "Stevie & I and Tina leaving by 3:35 for Toronto, closing house."

If, however, my uncle said little about the house, it was obvious, from the entries, it was because he was more preoccupied with the garden and with fishing and sailing. On Saturday, June 6: "Jones and I planted peas, sugar beets, I planted musk melon. June 7. Transplanted cabbages. . . . weather beautiful but a little cool." (He faithfully recorded the weather almost every day.) "Fresh beets Monday" was the only event worth recording one week. "July 1, Thurs. Ideal weather. asparagus going strong. peas full..." (I cannot make out the word here) "and . . . then crop young beets. Strawberries in heaps. Dry heat (July 6) fished once off point. Paul C. one bass." Wednesday, July 14 opened with high drama, apparently: "Terrific thunderstorm in afternoon; Jones & horses soused in garden. Jimmy Eakins arrived 9:30." He continued without a break. "Jimmy & I finished on Thursday under shelter . . . heavy wind . . . broke peak halliard. No fish. Jones planted 3 rows of beans and 2 of peas." So the fisherman's and sailor's disappointment was, perhaps, cancelled by the gardener's satisfaction. On July 27 it was worth recording that "Tina caught a very large Bass under Hewards Point a second broke her line."

Tina glowed when I told her of coming across this item. "Oh, dear," she said, "we were all so happy." Then she went on reminiscing about those days, and the early days (she joined Uncle Stephen's household around 1933, she told me). "It was such a happy house," she said. "We were always laughing, all of us . . . Sure, he had a temper, it was terrible sometimes, but it never lasted long. And you might be mad, but you got over it, because it was just his way, and he was so good to us." Tina said that at one time she and her five brothers were all working for my uncle. Laughing about one of my uncle's rages, she recounted the time her brother, Valmond, dented the car. "Mr. Leacock said, 'You get off my property, and don't ever come back,' " Tina related. "So

Valmond went downtown and stayed at the hotel; he was having a good time, and when he came for his clothes I asked him to come back. He said, 'Not me, never! He can't speak to me like that!' So I went to Mr. Leacock," Tina continued, "and I said, 'If my brother leaves here, and I never see him again, it's all your fault.' So when he saw how badly I felt he sent for Valmond and apologized to him and said, 'You know I didn't mean it. We can't do without you.' " Apparently Valmond made my uncle eat humble pie, and refused at first to return, but finally he gave in and came back.

"He was so wonderful to Kelly and me!" Tina sighed. "He used to lend us the car so often." "To go into Orillia, you mean?" I asked. "Orillia!" laughed Tina. "He let us take it on our holidays, to go down to New Brunswick."

The journal tells of Uncle George and Mary dropping in with the two little English girls who stayed with them during the war; of Aunt Dot coming several times; of Bâ (his affectionate name for my cousin Barbara who lived in Syracuse, New York after her marriage) and her little girl, Nancy, whom my uncle adored. He tells of Stevie's "other grandmother" (as we called her), Mrs. Hamilton, spending the weekend with them; of fishing with old friends like Aubrey Morphey and Charlie Fairweather. And of peas and cabbages, melons and strawberries that were, obviously, never less than perfect.

Fish and friends, strawberries and water melons, windstorms and a fall of guests from Montreal, the horses and the sailboat, family and foreigners – all are thrown in together, recorded along with the price he got for his peas, and the number of bass a guest caught from the point. Written very fast (the words often run together, as they do in his manuscripts) with, very obviously, whatever pen he could lay hands on.

A disorderly hodge-podge, disappointing to his historian?

No, not at all . . . a sample of the fabric of a life that was, as far as my uncle could control it, exactly the life he wished to lead. A life close to the earth and the water and the elements, in a house that might, perhaps, evidence lack of attention to the state of its physical health, but which was warm with love and friendship, as close as he could make it to the house "you can all come to." A house not perhaps, in all its physical details, the house he dreamed of that long-ago day when he bought the land on which it stood, but much closer, in essence, to his dream than most men achieve. Walls still echoing with laughter, though perhaps a little quieter now, waters still smiling in spite of occasional storms, a land still generous ... and a man growing old but still strong, and sharing his enjoyment of life with those he loved.

11

An Expedition to the Farm

And then, one summer's day, my uncle took us all to the farm at Egypt.

This farm had been my uncle's home for most of his childhood. His mother brought him there from England when he was six, together with his two older and two younger brothers and his sister. The remaining five of the eleven children were born there, and my mother was the youngest child.

The farm was four miles back from Lake Simcoe . . . four very long miles. According to my mother, Uncle Stephen accurately described it as being "in the middle of nowhere."

The day Uncle Stephen decided to take us there was as hot and breathless as, it seems to me, a day can be nowhere else in the world except in August, and in Ontario.

When I was a child, it seemed all August days were hot. So sullen and sticky that one could believe that God had gone to the other side of the world and forgotten his suffering children. Day after day he left a merciless, molten copper sun hanging in the sky, and fiery moons burned by night. Day after day the heat would continue, lasting for as long as a month, with not even the slightest breath of wind to stir the trees and grasses, or the waters of the lake and the river.

I can remember that in August the needles on the pine-trees in the lane behind my granny's cottage, and the flat-fingered leaves of the cedars in the high hedge, lost their shiny green, and were coated with the grey dust of the road. The leaves of the acacias wilted, and no longer sifted the pale-green light through their almond-shaped lozenges; their clusters hung limp as chicken-feather dusters and, like dusters, they, too, gathered dust.

We no longer played in the lane. The acacia houses stood untenanted, and the tall grass tunnels through which, as pirates, we had hurried, secretly, from the leafy council chambers of the acacias to our forbidden caves in the sand cliffs. The drying grasses of their inner walls grew brittle and crumbled. Field mice and rabbits were quite safe there now.

In the cliffs, the swifts took over our caves, pitting roofs and walls with their own apartments, fleeing, twittering, as the dry sands crumbled and gave way in the heat.

For the short time, in early morning and in the evening, which we children spent on land, we did not play. It was too hot. The little girls' hair became moist at the temples, and our mother braided it into pigtails, which she skewered on the tops of our heads, to keep the heat of our heavy manes away from our necks and shoulders. Beads of sweat stood out on Stephen's and Dickie's and David's foreheads, and ran down their noses, and dark damp patches spread across the shoulders of their cotton jerseys, and under their arms. They were compelled to wear hats all day, and beneath their chins, even when the elastic was loose, red gashes of prickly heat appeared.

We longed for water, but the pipe which ran out into the lake lay very close to the surface of the turgid water now, and the pump must be primed. Even then, and only after hoarse, rasping protest, it dribbled out a thin and insufficient stream. And this scant yield was tepid and stale.

Oh, to thrust our hot faces, as in July, beneath its ice-cold, breath-taking gush! To take its fierce, frigid blast head-on! To come up gasping, with faces, hair, even our clothes drenched and cool.

We longed for water, but we could get no surcease from these grudging drops.

The lake, of course, afforded some relief. But not enough. Always shallow in front of Granny's cottage, the water now went down,

down, down each day, till it was only thigh-high where it had been above our waists. It was warm, too, and as the sun beat down it became like the water in the bathtub in winter; heavy and dull.

Each day the lake went a little further down. All along the shore, the rocks bore ugly grey and brown marks to show the lowering level. Each day another line where, in July, crayfish had nosed against the bright green and pink and black quartz, and where, when the waves danced high, there had been tantalizing glimpses of even more brilliant hues, framed, for delirious split-seconds, with white foam and breaking bubbles.

Nor could you walk on the rocks now, they were so hot.

On the river, and even near the shore of the lake, an ugly green blanket of algae grew each day a little larger, turning our beloved lake into an ugly, tortured thing.

We were made to wear sun-hats when we went into the water, and sometimes jerseys as well, to protect our shoulders from the sun.

Nor could we go sailing. The *West Wind* lay in Mossington's Boathouse, and Uncle Charlie told us that there was green scum growing on her bottom. No sailing, for there was no wind, not any day, nor any evening. And it was much, much too hot to go up the river in the canoe.

Even the nights were often so hot we could not sleep. We bickered and whispered in the dark, were spanked or scolded, and our tired weeping and whimpering made the night seem even hotter. The screen doors banged often and bare feet padded across the floor and out to the closet, as restless children sought any excuse to leave their rumpled beds. Mothers brought drinks of water and scoldings to the sleepless ones. Even when we slept, it was so lightly that we awoke tired and cross.

Too tired to play, we lolled about and looked listlessly at our books, or told each other fearful tales of dogs gone mad in dog days. We looked anxiously at Jake, whose sides heaved in the heat, and from whose huge, fanged jaws ran steady rivulets of drool. His tongue and gums looked very pink, almost red, and his glistening white teeth looked cruelly sharp. Granny stayed at her house in Sutton, for the heat always affected her, and the little maid brought

Jake, like a child, to the lake to swim. Without his mistress' restraining influence, who knew what a heat-maddened Airedale might do? We even feared ancient Tuck, the Sibbald's collie, who padded slowly beneath the buggy from the Hall, seeking shade from the sun. We had heard that squirrels and chipmunks could also go mad in dog days, and attack children.

And once two copper-coloured snakes appeared on the bank, a hitherto unknown phenomena at Granny's cottage. We felt the season to be full of menace.

It was August, and dog days, and what possessed Uncle Stephen to take us inland in such weather?

What, at any time, and in any weather, for that matter, was the point in this visit to the past? Now, perhaps, I have come to understand something of his motives. But let me first tell you what I recall of that trip to Egypt. Afterwards, we will take a look at some of the things that happened to my uncle during his boyhood in "the middle of nowhere."

The day, as I said, was hot.

We could not have slept well, for we dawdled over our breakfast, not caring greatly when we got into our bathing things and sun hats, casting lacklustre eyes on the still, stale lake. The water, we knew, would not be cool. We were in no hurry for the day to begin.

So we reacted with less protest than usual when Uncle Stephen appeared with his announcement that it was "Ho! for the farm!" I suppose we may even have welcomed the prospect; we had heard so much from our parents about the farm at Egypt, scene of heroic and comic antics of our hero-uncles, seat of strange, hinted-at horrors. We had often asked to be taken there.

Uncle Stephen appeared at the cottage in the early forenoon. He had with him Stevie and the driver of the car. (Freddy Pellatt, Stevie and I lately figured it must have been.)

Uncle Teddy and Aunt Gypsy, with Peter and Joan, were also on the expedition, and the local contingent included Aunt Carrie, with David and Dora, and Uncle Charlie. Then there was my mother with Stephen and Dickie, Margaret and myself, and my cousin Agnes, of course.

I recall a buzz of excitement amongst us as the expedition of three cars started along the Lakeshore Road. Yes, and even a certain pride as cottagers along the way looked up at our *entourage*. Let *them* get through the monotony of yet another August day – *we* were adventure-bound.

We left them sitting on their verandahs, or trudging along the road to go bathing in the hot, dull lake, while we headed bravely, in our glistening chariots, directly due south. Egypt lies inland from the lake some four or five miles and, give or take a few turns and twists, the road runs almost perpendicular to the lakeshore.

I do not know how it is now, maybe there is a super-highway running back to Egypt, though I doubt it. But I know that when we drove there that long-ago day, it was a very narrow road, with the only "improvement" a dubious one – sharp gravel filling the deepest ruts and pot-holes.

There were still even some stretches of "corduroy" road. That is, narrow logs laid across the road and covered with earth. This detail caused some delight and laughter amongst our elders. They reminded each other of how Granny would caution them to "hold on" as they hit these rough, bumpy stretches, and they marvelled that this antique bit of road-building should still be in existence.

Corduroy road was, I suppose, the only way, and a good one, in the early days, when this part of Ontario was being opened up, to maintain a stretch of road which ran through low, boggy land, and to ensure passage during the spring season, when a dirt road could be completely washed out. I recall my mother telling us that on several springs, when the rains were particularly heavy, or when thawing snows loosed a great flood, the bog beneath the corduroy rose into a veritable lake, and the wooden road swung, like a bridge, over the water. Then, she said, the older children would have to get out of the buggy, and one of the boys would carefully lead Cuff, the nervous mare, across the wet, slippery logs, now almost bare of their dirt blanket.

We passed over a length of this corduroy road shortly after we left the church. It runs (or ran then) through a great, woody marsh. The branches of the trees almost met over the tops of the cars, and made a long, cool tunnel for us. The logs were covered, as our mother had told us they often were in summer, with a broadloom of green moss; and even though we could scarcely speak for the rough bumping we got (this with pneumatic tires, so imagine how rough the logs would have been beneath steel-rimmed buggy wheels!), we laughed at such an exotic experience and I, at least, already looked forward to telling playmates in Belleville about it.

The road, as I say, was apparently scarcely changed since the days when Uncle Stephen and his mother and brothers and sisters used to drive old Cuff and her sleighful or buggy-load down to the lakeshore. And many years later, when my husband and I drove *our* children up to see the farm, the road was still narrow and untarred, with the deep ruts casually filled with gravel, and the corduroy road still running through the marsh.

Then the swamp ended. We emerged from the tunnel of trees, left the bumpy bit of corduroy, and hit the narrow trail through the open fields again. There were no cool trees to shade us now. As I recall, no trees at all along the way, except the scrubby, dust-coated hawthorns and, in the distance, an occasional elm standing tall and lofty in the middle of a field. Sheep and cattle crouched in the purple lake of shade provided by its broad umbrella. I fancy there must have been threshers and their wagons and horses in the fields, for this was the threshing season. Present, also, would have been the rickety windmills of the hayrack, which the farmer then used to draw through the fields, with the men pitching their forkloads of grain up into their great skeletons of arms.

I recall that the whole country seemed very still, as in a dream. The cattle and the sheep did not move beneath the elms, or in the shadow of the hedges. We met no other cars on the road. After all, there were no other hamlets on the way, and the few farmers who lived at Egypt had their haying to do. On Sunday they would drive down to church, but now they had no reason to venture abroad. So the road was empty, although far ahead of us a spiral of dust hung in the air, like the Hiroshima mushroom, to show that a car had gone on before us. It hung there for a long, long time, with no sign of the car, so it must have passed many minutes before.

There was dust everywhere. Fine, filthy grey dust. It lay in a thick blanket over the hard, baked earth-bed of the road. It rose in clouds, almost before our tires touched it. It enveloped the cars, coating the windshields, so that we had to stop every now and then to wipe them clean. The cars were open, of course, and the dust came into them, making us choke, and rub our eyes. Our hands were grimy with dust, and in front of me one of my boy cousins wore a broad collar of dust above his jersey. My mother had tied a blue polka-dotted scarf about her curly brown-blonde hair, to keep it clean, and, in the car ahead, Aunt Gypsy, driving, wore a broad-brimmed white straw hat.

Occasional spurts of gravel flew from their caches in the potholes. Hitting the road, they raised their own small spirals of dust.

We grew thirsty, but were told to wait until we got to the farm. We became even more excited, then, at the prospect of the farmhouse pump. In spite of the dust and the heat, we were lively and happy.

So, too, were the grown-ups. Aunt Carrie and Mother chatted together, breaking off every few minutes to point out some special spot or event on the journey. "Here's the place where Cuff lost her shoe!" one of them would cry. And "Children! Here's where Teddy and George used to have to get out and walk behind the sleigh!" (This was a familiar legend – the fact that in winter, when the snow was heavy, the boys and older children would lighten the load by walking alongside the sleigh, while Granny drove, with my mother and perhaps Aunt Dot and Aunt Carrie or Maymee beside her.)

Then there were the places where Cuff had to be dug out of the snow – poor Cuff, there were so many of them that I wonder the good old mare even had the courage to start out on a winter's journey to Sutton or the Hall. There was the spot where Aunt

Missie's straw hat, a treasured gift from London, had blown off, and had been retrieved from a bramble bush. There was the place where Aunt Dot's doll had cracked its face on the side of the buggy because of a rough jolt. There was the spot where my mother, on a winter night, noticing the stars for the first time, had said, "Look, mother, there are holes in the sky!" "Mother had laughed," wrote my own mother, many years later, "and, drawing the big fur robe around me she said, 'Why, those are stars, dear.'"

With so much history, and so many diversions, and the longed-for legend about to break, we did not really mind the heat and the dust. Faster, faster, Uncle Stephen, dear leader, please let us go faster, we yearn for the promised land.

Then, at last, a turn off the road, a drive up along a narrow lane fenced with farm wire, and we were there.

Out of the cars we tumbled, and had burst across the land before the engines had ceased chortling, and the drivers had disembarked. The farm, the farm, we had come to see the farm!

In *The Boy I Left Behind Me* my uncle described his boyhood home as

> The damndest place I ever saw. . . . Someone had built a cedar-log house and then covered it round with clapboard, and then someone else had added three rooms stuck along the front with more clapboard, effectually keeping all the sunlight out. Even towards the sunset there were no windows, only the half glass top of a side door. A cookhouse and a woodshed were stuck on behind.

When we piled out of the cars that August day, there it stood. On the brow of the hill – as we had been told it did – and roughcast, with very few trees about it.

But what shocked us into complete silence was the size of the place. How could this tiny box have contained a parlour and a night nursery and a day nursery, and bedrooms, and the big kitchen about which we had so often heard? We stared in dumb astonishment.

The grown-ups appeared to be in an equal state of shock. They too could only stare in astonishment at the little, decaying house – no longer laughing or even talking. And Uncle Stephen the leader – the promoter, as it were, of the farm – said not a word. He just stood there, drawing slowly on his pipe several times and surveying the ruin.

My mother told me afterwards that she had expected the place to look a lot smaller than she remembered it. Reality often reveals childhood memories of mansions to be little more than cottages. But surely the farm couldn't have been *this much smaller?*

Then Uncle Stephen said, "Why, part of it is gone! This is only the new part!"

They all laughed then, and someone else joined in, agreeing, "Of course, they must have torn down the old part." Then everyone felt better, and they started to walk about the house, which was deserted, and so securely locked up that I cannot even remember getting a glimpse inside. I remember wondering at the fact that there seemed to be no windows, except for the small oblong of glass in the side door, which was so high up that even my grandmother would have had to stand on tip toes to see through it. This door led, my mother told us, into the kitchen. Beside it was a gnarled old lilac tree. "Aunt Dot's lilac tree," cried Mother happily. "It came into bloom the day she was born!"

The grown-ups began, then, to search for clues and remnants of their old home. The children scattered, too, exploring on their own. The pump was forgotten, which was just as well, because it stood rusty and looking as if it had not been used since the Leacocks had left, and the boards over the well were so rotten that they might have given way to the touch of even a child's foot.

They found the outlines of the foundations of the missing house. "Here is where the passageway must have been," decided Aunt Carrie; and once again they were off, laughing and chattering happily together.

"Charlie, remember how we used to skate down the passageway?" Uncle Stephen chuckled, taking his pipe from his mouth.

"And mother used to scold us, and say we would ruin the floor?"

joined in Uncle Charlie. At which they all laughed uproariously. And even we older children could see how absurd a reprimand this would have been. Most of us were only too familiar with old houses, to whose splintered pine floors no skate could possibly do any further damage.

We were also used to long, cold passageways. (God knows, such structures as the farm sprang not from an architect's board!) The builders of the day were very fond of joining together several successive additions to a house by such passages, much in the same way as a sloppy woman might hold together her costume with safety pins, or I might staple together the pages of a manuscript.

As a result, no two parts of any given house ever seemed to be on the same level, and the passages themselves were always windowless and dark. One of the first things a child learned was to feel for the floor before he entered or left a passageway. There was always at least one step up or down – and the unwary or the careless were in for a nasty prat-fall, or, at very least, a stubbed toe. Our house in Belleville, only a few decades less venerable than this farmhouse, had several such pasages. They were cold enough for your breath to turn to steam, and on your way to the bathroom you huddled deep into your dressing-gown and, returning, dived thankfully under the warm covers of your bed.

It is true that our passageways in Belleville were not cold enough for ice to form on their boards. But then that house had a furnace, whereas the farm at Egypt was heated entirely by fireplaces and stoves. ("Nine of them, I believe there were," groaned my uncle, recalling the hours of woodchopping it took to keep them stoked.) So I can well believe that the boys could skate in the freezing passage which joined the night and day nurseries to that part of the house which contained the parlour and kitchen. (Whether they actually flooded the passageway to make their "rink," or whether snow blew in through the thin walls to form a frozen surface, I do not know.)

"And remember how we used to break the ice in the water pitcher before we could wash in the morning?" chimed in Aunt Carrie, as happily as if she were recalling some rare treat.

"And Granny said there were always frost flowers on the windows of her bedroom," one of us piped up.

"Yes! Yes! Yes! Where's the window with the frost flowers?" demanded Agnes. "Granny says there were so many frost flowers you couldn't see out. Granny said it was so dark inside in the morning, you had to have candles."

"Dark it was," agreed Uncle Teddy. "But not just the frost. The snowdrifts were so high that they came up over the window. Remember, Stephen?"

But Uncle Stephen didn't answer. He appeared to be very intent upon lighting his pipe. I noticed this, because his silence acted as a sudden brake on the excitement that had been generated amongst the rest of us. We children looked up at him, expecting he was going to tell us some story about the snow and the frost, but then my mother said, a little too quickly, "Stephen, why don't you show the boys the barn?" And my uncle replied, as if glad to change the subject, "Yes, come along, boys," and led the boys, with the girls following of course, down the slope to the right of the house in search of the barn. Soon he and the other two uncles were hunting for their initials, which they had carved so long ago in the logs of the low cowshed.

We examined the initials in the cowshed. We found the remains of what my mother told us was her father's flower-garden. ("Your father was a wonderful gardener," my mother recalled Granny telling her. Then Mother went on to say, "I remember the garden fenced in between the house and the orchard by a picket fence, [with] an old-fashioned catch on the little gate. . . . Sometimes on a still fall day mother would take my sister Dot and me through the gate and walk among the fruit trees, and pick the purple grapes that hung in heavy clusters from the vines. Mother would talk to us of father, and then grow silent, and hurry us out of the garden and back to the house, as if she could not stay another minute.")

Peter's garden was now a tangle of weeds, with the roses all gone to seed.

Full of curiosity, we continued exploring. We found a small fenced-off plot beyond the garden which contained two tombstones. They marked the graves of settlers who had lived on the farm before the Leacocks came. We gaped at the hummocky field which had been a cricket pitch for my uncle and his brothers. (Not so long ago, I stood on the smooth green of Hambledon Downs, where the Leacock brothers had first played the noble game, and which had inspired the sorry substitute at Egypt, and I marvelled at the bravery of those small English boys.)

Somehow, I lost track of Uncle Stephen after he took the boys down to the cowshed. Generally, in his role of omnipotent stage manager, he was all over the place, acting as cheer leader, whipping up enthusiasm, engineering responses, volubly delighted with his latest "project."

But during that visit to Egypt I recall no such evidence of his usual high spirits. Whether we went to sit in the car while we explored, or became engrossed in conversation with Uncle Teddy and Uncle Charlie, I do not remember. All that I can recall is that when the heat, and the continuous buzzing torment of the big, dirty horse-flies began to curb our enthusiasm, and we started asking when we could go home, Uncle Stephen made no objection.

So we all clambered back into the cars and soon were once more raising clouds of dust on the road that led, mercifully, away from Egypt, away from the land of Back-Then. Away – although I was not to divine this for many years – from a night when frost flowers were hideous in their blossoming, and snowdrifts became a refuge from terror.

12

Frost Flowers in the Night

What was in my uncle's mind, when he decided to take us to the farm?

Why should he want to take us there at any time, and in any weather?

But to choose that August day, of all days, when the thermometer must have stood at 80° or even higher.

So hot and dry, that journey to the middle of nowhere.

So dry, so dusty, so parched, that pilgrimage to the land of Back-Then.

So parched, that pilgrimage, and so utterly without reward.

Pilgrimage? – Or punishment, perhaps.

I thought of that journey to the farm so often as I grew older. It bobbed up every now and then in my thoughts as every unsolved riddle must.

I thought of it so often, and still did not know the answer.

Nor, when I looked back and remembered my uncle that day, did I believe that *he* knew why he went.

Yet he was in some way compelled to go, and compelled to take us all with him . . . his own son, all the brothers and sisters he could gather, and their sons and daughters.

Most certainly Uncle Stephen had a motive in making the expedition. He loved, as I have remarked before, to play God, or the omnipotent stage manager; to pick us up and put us into a scene. And almost always the scene was a happy one, at least in his conception of it.

That it was necessary for us to go with him to Egypt – that is easy to understand.

And if the pilgrimage turned out to be a punishment to him – as there were signs that it did – I do not think he foresaw that it would so affect him.

In retrospect, it seems to me that Uncle Stephen had always shown a rather odd attitude toward the farm . . . in his writings and in actual conversation.

He joked about it in his writings, but the jokes were clumsy. They seemed forced. Moreover, if one added up several references, one came away with the distinct impression that he hated the farm.

If he had ever expressed outspoken hatred . . . the kind of frank loathing which my mother felt, not only for her own home, but for all farms and farming . . . he might not have aroused the curiosity of his critics and biographers.

He joked, too, when he talked about the farm. But again the clumsiness, a feeling that the joke was out of place. Why make a joke, if it wasn't a good joke? It wasn't like him.

So there was always the question mark. What was he really saying? What did he really feel? Was he being purposefully (or even unconsciously) vague when he talked about Egypt? Was he trying to conceal some secret hurt, some wound whose nature even he did not fully realize?

I am not pretending that as a child I was even faintly aware of all these subtleties. My slight sense of puzzlement at his attitude during our visit was soon swallowed up in the excitement of getting back to the lake. It was only much later when, grown up, I sometimes thought back to that day that I began to think how obscure his motives had been for dragging us away on that pilgrimage. And it was many, many years before it occurred to me that Uncle Stephen's behaviour on that occasion did, perhaps, provide a clue to how he really felt about both the place and the early years of his boyhood.

In the early years, of course, I knew very little about the events that had led up to my grandparents' separation. I knew that the last years on the farm had been unhappy ones, and that the farm itself had been going to rack and ruin. But it was not until I was a lot older that I finally heard the exact events of the last chapter of their lives together, and understood why the mention of frost-flowers traced on a window-pane, and of white snow drifted against the wall of the house should erase the laughter from my uncle's face, and cast him into silence.

There are a number of references in Uncle Stephen's writing to the "separation" between his parents. In his earlier books he tried to make light of it. Even my own mother attempted a humorous touch when she commented, "Father was a luxury Mother could no longer afford."

It all sounds very sensible, doesn't it? A quiet, reasonable discussion: "Let's be adult," says Agnes to Peter. "Let us agree to separate." A civilized decision. Everybody being decent all round. The kind of thing that happens every day in our modern world. And the manly boy, assisting his father with his packing and lovingly, regretfully, putting him on the train.

But let us look a little deeper. My uncle assumed that would-be-humorous attitude to his father's departure during the period when my grandmother was still living in Sutton, among people to whom memories of her former unhappy life had already become dim. It could have been very hurtful to her, if the whole truth had been dragged out into the open at that time. ("Tell me, Mrs. Leacock, do you ever hear from yer man?" an officious farmer's wife once asked my grandmother. "And," says Uncle George, who was with my grandmother at the time, "Mother sat in the buggy, looking straight ahead of her, and her back straight as a whip, never saying a word until we were home again.")

I also believe that Uncle Stephen himself would have found it painful to talk about the real reasons for his parents' separation. Yet every time that he returned to the event in his writing, he moved a little closer to the stark truth. There is very little attempt to gloss over the facts in *The Boy I Left Behind Me:*

"My father, as he drank more, changed towards us from a superman and a hero into a tyrant, from easy and kind to fits of brutality."

That states the case plainly enough. It is also clear that the change in my grandfather's behaviour was a gradual process, taking place over a period of years. And the "brutality" to which Uncle Stephen refers was, I know, physical – and it was exercised against my grandmother, as well as against the children.

One does not need, after all, a great deal of imagination, to realize how such an atmosphere must have affected the boy, Stephen. He might indeed eat well enough and have shoes upon his feet. He might go to the little red schoolhouse and later, thanks to his mother's foresight, be taught by the brilliant young scholar who became their private tutor. He might pore over books from England, and be constantly encouraged and inspired by a mother who was not only well-educated, but exceptionally witty and intelligent.

Ah yes, but while he scanned his Virgil, while he juggled his sums, while he observed the beauty of the surrounding country and far-off Lake Simcoe, he must also have been learning a lesson in practical economics. *Ergo*: how, if the farmer drinks, can the farm flourish? Tell me, dear books, how are we to eat tomorrow if my father grows no crops today? Riddle me that riddle.

Of course, in the early years of the farm's decline, the truth was concealed from the children. As Uncle Stephen says:

> All this time, although we didn't know, for my mother kept it hidden from us, at intervals my father drank, drove away to the village in the evening to return late at night after we were in bed, or lay round the farm too tired to work, and we thought it was the sun. And the more he drank, the more the farm slid sideways and downhill, and the more the cloud of debt, of unpaid bills, shadowed it over, and the deeper the shadow fell, the more he drank. [This is from *The Boy I Left Behind Me.*]

Inevitably, however, Stephen began to realize what was really happening. He might drift off to sleep dreaming of Ulysses and his adventures, but he would wake to the shouting of an angry drunkard, and to his mother's weeping. And again he might lie listening to his baby sister, rudely awakened, crying in the night. Then, with eyes still smarting from lack of sleep, he might forsake his books and go out to clean the cowshed and milk the cows, because he knew that his father, whom he had brought home unconscious with drink from the Sutton public house, most certainly would not attend to these tasks. He would do what he could for his mother, watching her grow old from repeated and unwilling child-bearing, and from worry. But at all times he would also be forced to meet her proud defence, her refusal to admit to the hopelessness of her husband's state.

It is very likely the boy would also observe that if his mother *did* attempt to protest to her husband about his behaviour, Peter would pour his troubles into other, more sympathetic ears – those of the children's nursemaid. (A succession of them, I suspect.) Of one of them, at least, I have heard that my proud grandmother, when she complained to the girl about her neglect of the baby, was forced to endure her boasts that "the master had said she could leave the child's care to its mother."

My Uncle Stephen, like all my uncles, was naturally gallant and chivalrous from the time he was a little boy. And he adored his mother. What he must have gone through as he watched the suffering she endured is almost beyond imagination. The picture I have drawn only hints at the terror and despair which must have filled that lonely house for most of the years of his boyhood.

Then, finally, it came to an end – but not by virtue of any civilized conversation between a man and a woman agreeing to abandon a marriage that was beyond repair. No, this last chapter was quite different from what you may have imagined.

All the details I do not know. I do know, however, that one December night my uncle woke yet again to furious oaths, to my grandmother's frightened screams, and the mewling of my mother, then a tiny baby. There was a knife in my grandfather's hand and, in order to escape him, my grandmother snatched the child from the cradle and leapt through the window into the snowdrifts outside.

Stephen helped my grandmother out of the drift and made her dress in warm clothes, bundling the two smaller girls into their clothing as well. Then he hitched old Cuff to the sleigh and drove them down to Eildon Hall, which was four miles away. There they stayed for several days, until he had got his father out of the house, driven him into Sutton and sent him away. As some member of my family apparently told Ralph L. Curry, who recounts this episode in his book, *Stephen Leacock, Humorist and Humanist*, the boy, horsewhip in hand, said to his father, "If you ever come back, I will kill you."

Now do you see how it was?

The pretty frost flowers on the window ... and a terrified woman struggling to get it open. A candle lighting the dark downstairs bedroom ... and the flash of a knife-blade in its light. Innocent white snow falling outside ... drifting against the farmhouse wall ... piling up for Christmas ... piling up to make a soft blanket for a woman to leap into. Snow over the fields and over the road, and "Jingle bells! Jingle bells! Jingle all the way. Oh, what fun it is to ride ...." Faster, faster, dear Cuff, and drive forever if we must, till we have gone so many, many years and miles from here that we may never have to return to the drunken wreck who was once my hero, who is forever my father; to the smug nursemaid who mocked my mother; to the fields which will not yield, no matter how rich next summer may be; to the house which is so far away from England; to the farm at Egypt, the old farm I'll write about, the hated farm, the constant core of my incurably scarred heart.

I have, of course, read a great deal into this narrative, and into my uncle's thoughts that I could not possibly know. But the events which I have related were real, and I know the kind of boy and man he was, from my mother, from my grandmother, from the others, and from my own observation. I think I must be very close to the mark when I imagine what must have been in the sixteen-year-old boy's mind on that long, cold drive away from the farm. I think I know why he could not, without pain, dwell upon frost flowers and snowdrifts, and that long-ago December night.

13

...and Sunlight Through the Clouds

Of course, there had not always been clouds at the farm in Egypt. It was not all an atmosphere of drunken tantrums, and nights of terror.

My uncle has written, in *The Boy I Left Behind Me*, of the family's arrival at their new home – and of their first sight of Sutton – "... two mills, two churches, and quite a main street, with three taverns." He goes on to say, "My father told us that this was our own village, a gift very lightly received by us children after memories of Portchester and Liverpool."

Then on they drove, "up a great hill with more farmhouses, and so across some fields, to a great wind-swept hill space with a jumble of frame buildings and log barns and out-houses, and there we were at the old farm, on a six-year unbroken sentence."

No doubt, the hearts of both Agnes and Peter Leacock must have sunk when they first caught a glimpse of their new home. One of Stephen's historians has remarked that "it was a comfortable house by the standards of the time." That is all very well, but he was judging it by the standards of other Canadian settlers in their immediate neighbourhood. Also, from what I have seen of its remains, it was by no means as comfortable, nor in any way as gracious a house as those belonging to the Leacock's neighbours, the Sibbalds, the Mossingtons, the Andersons, and the other gentlemen settlers near or around the lakeshore. It was a poor thing indeed compared to the house which my paternal great-great grandfather built on the London road, or the Leacock and Butler homes in

England. And please also consider that my grandparents and their family did not have the comfortable distance of Uncle Stephen's biographer from which to gain a perspective.

Nevertheless, the Leacocks could not have been wholly unhappy. At least they were together again with their children, and their own home. They were young and strong, Canada was the land of opportunity. They had no fears; and if there was some nagging doubt about the failure in South Africa, and the failure in Kansas, why, this was different. They were older now, and these past experiences could be useful. So let ice freeze on the window panes, let the winds howl outside the farmhouse, let the stoves grumble for more wood — within, their home was filled with laughter and song and high spirits. Close the door on the snow and the ice. It is warm and safe inside.

For the boy Stephen and his brothers and sister, at least the first months on the farm must have been a great adventure.

There were new games to play. The six-year-old immigrant and his brothers must often have forgotten their homesickness for Hampshire in the thrill of discovering their new home. Broad fields upon which to imagine whole armies at war; woods as dense as the thickest jungles Robinson Crusoe ever trod, inhabited, too, by wildcats, very real and therefore much more thrilling than the fiercest beasts with which their imaginings could have infested the gentle copse behind the cottage at Swanmore, or beyond the battlements of Portchester Castle. There were occasional meetings with the Redskins, disappointingly minus war paint and feathers, it is true, but as taciturn and stone-faced as in any storybook; there was the challenge of playing cricket on these hummocky savage fields; there was the strangeness of the two tombstones behind the barns, with their chilling reminder of lives spun out before their own on these isolated acres.

There were the Sunday treats. To crown all these pleasures, on Sundays old Tommy, the hired man, hitched up Collar and Cuff, and Papa and Mama took their family to Sibbald's Church ... an event in which the ancillary pleasures greatly outweighed the unpleasantness of sitting still for an hour and a half during the service. There was the four-mile drive, to begin with – in later years a hardship, but, when the children were smaller, a taste of the big, wide world; and to young Missie, who wore to church a velvet hat trimmed with ostrich plumes (sent her by her doting Aunt Kitty Leacock), this opportunity alone was reason enough to love church-going.

There was sociability. During the service they could covertly signal their new friends, the Hett boys and girls (Mrs. Hett, a widow, had been a Sibbald before her marriage). Later, outside the church, came the reunion, after a week's separation, and the forging of friendships which were to last a lifetime. Also after the service came the greatest reunion of all – with the water, with their new love, Lake Simcoe. As Stephen Leacock was to later write, in *The Boy I Left Behind Me*: "The whole point of our going to church on the lake shore on summer mornings was that we were allowed, by a special dispensation from the awful Sunday rules we were brought up on, to go in for a swim and to stick around beside the lake for an hour or so." (The summer Stephen was eleven, the Leacocks rented a down-at-heel parsonage near the lake, and the children "like Viking children back to the sea," as my uncle wrote, cast themselves into a two-month Bacchanalia of water pleasures: swimming, diving, wading, raft-building, raft-sailing, sailboating, canoeing, rowboating, picnics in the daytime and bonfires by the night ... the whole bit which we, a generation later, picked up and pursued with the same passionate fervour.)

There were the winter games. And then, of course, for the Leacock children, there was their new country's especial gift, the white winter. Later, Stephen Leacock might write of the desperate loneliness of winter on the farm, but to boys of six and eight and nine, the boundaries of their world were limited to the distance their small legs could walk. And here, quite literally on their doorsteps,

Heaven spread a soft white blanket of snow. Snow, upon which to make angel patterns. Snow upon which to play Fox and Geese. Snow for constructing forts and castles. Snow to provide ammunition for three months of battles. Snow upon the fields, across which to track the small wild creatures; to discover field mice tenting out among the dried weeds, or the hickety-pickety of the wild bunny's footsteps, his trail punctuated, to the great hilarity of the wicked boys, by frozen brown pellets.

Snow on the hills, down which to slide on their first sleighs; snow on the roads, and Collar and Cuff with bells a-jingle on their harnesses as the boys ran behind the sleigh.

Strange new snow-toys . . . skates and sleighs and ice-boats and snow-shoes.

Later, as the little sisters were born, and grew, they would make snow puddings and cupcakes of ice, using the tin pans from the kitchen for moulds, and Carrie, who was clever, would colour hers by mixing crepe paper in the slush before she packed it into the moulds, so that, on a flat snow table, within a snow igloo, her imaginary guests could sit down to raspberry or orange or lime-coloured desserts.

The little girls made angels too, and taught the baby (every two or three years, a new baby) to lie on its back, keep its feet together and wave its fat little arms back and forth to make wings; then on your feet again, Baby, and look! there's an angel in the snow — your angel!

And ice upon the ponds . . . a rink of thick frozen glass at their own doorstep, upon which to try their new skates; and, in the marshes, wafer-thin, brittle, flower-patterned ice about the reeds; and crystal clear ice to roof nature's aquarium, so that a small boy might watch, miraculously, small, bright green frogs and beetles move.

Indoors, Stephen's sisters played with the enormous doll's house a fond uncle had sent to Aunt Missie . . . a three-storey mansion, with about twenty rooms, each completely furnished, down to tiny wineglasses, silver forks and knives and fine china on the dinner table, a hand mirror and streamered straw hat on milady's dressing table, and chamberpots in the servant's attic bedrooms. It had a family of doll aristocrats and their servants, the former with elaborate changes of costume. My mother told me, when I was little, that the Prince of Wales (later Edward VII) had inspected the doll's house. I assumed that the Prince had dropped in at the farm for this express purpose, and was quite deflated to discover later that the "inspection" had taken place during Edward's opening of a trade fair, or whatever the Victorian equivalent of such an event might be; it was, I believe, in the Crystal Palace. Still, there was some comfort for me in the thought that the Prince had singled out Aunt Missie's doll's house for his attention; the most vainglorious of the Leacock children's playmates could not boast such regal interest in their toys.

The little girls also played with wax-faced dolls from England and cried when one especially cold morning they woke to find the pink wax cheeks cracked from the cold. (That same night, Mama's tortoise-shell bracelet cracked right in half; Mama heard the sound, and couldn't think what it was, but when, next day, she opened her jewel case to take out her big Scotch pebble brooch, there was the broken bracelet, with the silver filigree flowers and beetles torn from the rivets which had held them to the tortoise-shell.)

On very cold days in winter, the children stayed all day in the day nursery, poring over the latest *London Illustrated*. Or they painted pictures, or played on the splintered nursery floor with their lead soldiers. The little girls made doll's clothes, or dressed up in their mother's old party dresses; she let them play with a spray of pearls she had, long ago, worn in her hair when she was a young girl, going to dances, with cousin Tom Butler at Hamilton, or just for coming down to dinner at Brighton. The pearls broke off and fell through the cracks in the floor, but Mother only said, "Oh, dear, what a pity!" Sometimes, too, she would take out the big leather-covered jewel box that had been made for Aunt Kitty Leacock. The trays were lined with garnet-coloured velvet, and each tray was shaped to fit Aunt Kitty's jewelry – funny-shaped troughs for the big pendant earrings; long, shallow trenches for the bracelets and dog-collars; large and small lozenges into which once fitted Kitty's many brooches and clips.

There were "entertainments" at the school-house, too, to break the long shut-in winter season. My mother has left us an account of the Leacock children's share in one of these:

> The Christmas I was three there was, as usual, a concert at the school-house. Two of my older sisters were to take part in a "Rock-a-bye Baby" chorus. I think the older one was ten, the younger one eight. Dot and I, although not old enough to go to school, were to sing a duet, "The Three Little Kittens."
>
> The afternoon before the big event, dressed in our best navy velvet dresses with white lace collars, we stood by the piano in the sitting room to rehearse our "piece." The piano was a small "cottage piano" painted black with gold lines to trim and with gilt candle sticks in brass brackets over the keyboard. Mother struck the opening cord. "Now," she nodded encouragingly " 'Three Little Kittens. . . .' "
>
> Dot and I, one on each side of her, got off to a good start. We had the kittens right through the horror of the lost mittens, our "mews" were realistic enough to bring our cat in from the kitchen with a worried look on her face. But alas! the joy of finding the mittens put an end to my concert career. For, when I tried to purr there was only a spluttering sound. I tried again and again. The hissing sounds filled the room. Dot, who was purring beautifully, stopped short. "Go on, dear," Mother encouraged. "No! No!" Dot cried. "I won't sing with her, she can't purr!"; and though I burst into tears and Mother pleaded with her, no amount of coaxing would move her to another "Purr." Mother, realizing that further talking was useless, dried my tears and enlarged on the fact that anyway I was going to the concert, and would see the girls "Rock their dollies to sleep"....
>
> I don't remember . . . if the master of ceremonies announced that "Due to circumstances beyond our control, the

duet, 'Three Little Kittens,' by Dot and Daisy Leacock will not be sung, in its place we will have a piano solo by Dot Leacock." Dot who had taken lessons for about a year, played quite well, and "rendered" (the announcer's word) a little "piece" called "Chopsticks."

As a matter of fact, she had to "render" it twice, not really because of the applause but because of "technical difficulties." The platform had a curtain across it which, at a signal, was rolled up by one of the older pupils. When you saw the curtain rolling up you knew the stage was set with Dot at the piano. The teacher, in the wings, gave the signal for the curtain to roll, and for Dot to start playing. Both started at once, but alas, the curtain stuck! Not an unusual thing, as you know if you have ever run that sort of curtain. Dear little Dot, unconscious of what had happened, played happily on. "Out front" all that was seen was the bottom of the piano, the stool, and Dot's thin little legs, encased in black cashmere stockings with kid slippers on her feet.

"Ta la la, Ta la la," went the piano, while a frantic teacher and pupil worked at the pulley on the offending curtain. As suddenly as it had stuck the curtain began to roll, reaching the top just as the final cord of the tune was played. Dot slid off the stool and turned to make a little bow. The audience laughed and clapped and cried "Encore! Encore!"; At a sign from her teacher Dot climbed back on the stool and again "Chopsticks" filled the room; then, with another bow, the young performer walked off stage to join Mother and me in the hall. She was unconscious of what had occurred and not till "the boys" (our brothers) told her later, did she understand why she had had to "play her piece" twice.

Mother wanted to take us home then as it was growing late, but of course we had to stay to see our big sisters do their part. We waited impatiently till twelve little girls trouped onto the stage, each carrying a doll dressed in a long white dress (the fashion for babies in those days). I easily picked out my sisters, dressed alike in dark woolen dresses trimmed with velvet.

Maymee, the eight-year-old was a chubby, solemn little girl. She had beautiful chestnut-coloured hair which hung below her waist; she wore a wide black velvet ribbon round her head tied in a bow at the top. I think she was nervous for as the teacher started playing "Rock-a-Bye Baby" and the girls lined up in front, she moved very close to our older sister.

The little girls were all singing now, and were rocking the dolls back and forth. Maymee, who had little sense of rhythm, started rocking her baby out of turn. Being too close to her sister there was a terrific crash as the doll's heads came together. Maymee's doll got the worst of it and carried the marks all through her dolly life.

Yes, in the Leacock's early years at the farm, there was more sunlight than cloud. Even after my grandfather had left, there was still plenty of lightness of heart. (The Christmas concert I have just described took place after his departure.)

If, from the first, the farm did not show a profit, how were Peter and Agnes to realize that these were not just the venture's "growing pains"? Besides, they were both by nature easy-going and lighthearted. When Stephen, and the older children, many years later, spoke of their father during those early days, they drew a picture of a gay, witty and indulgent man. ("The most amusing man I have ever known," as Granny told my mother.) Like Granny, he used to read aloud to them ("Your father read aloud so well," my mother quotes Granny.) In those days he was a great hero to Stephen and his older brothers.

The farm must have been, in a way, a bit of a joke to Peter and Agnes. It must have been hard to take the roles of "The Farmer and his Wife" seriously; to believe that the game would not soon come to an end, and that they would not be back again in England, their real home. My mother used to tell me about the winter they spent in Toronto, whence they moved when Granny fell heir to a small legacy. The older children recalled it as a wonderful time, with Father and Mother going out to dinner parties and to the theatre, and the house on John Street filled with laughter and gaiety. I think it must have been about this time that they used to visit at The Grange, Mr. Goldwin Smith's home on Grange Road, which is now a part of the Ontario Art Gallery.

But, in spite of her enjoyment of gay times, my grandmother was never greatly concerned with material luxuries – a broken bracelet, pearls lost through the floor – "What a pity," was her usual response. My mother told of Uncle Stephen, home for the Christmas holidays, putting the silver butter dish on the stove to melt the butter, then becoming absorbed in conversation with one of his friends, and letting not only butter, but the silver butter dish melt away completely! "But Mother only said, 'Never mind, it was an accident' and I never heard her mention the matter again, although we did not get another silver butter dish, either." In the same account, Mother remarked on the gradual depletion of the table silverware – "the silver spoons and forks, etc., and the good china, went along on picnics as a matter of course . . . and gradually were lost or broken." I can well believe this, for Granny's furniture and other possessions in her Sutton house were certainly battle-scarred and shabby, and although her daughters, particularly my mother, seemed to be constantly refurbishing them and trying to bring them up to scratch, Granny seemed very little interested in this process, although grateful for their efforts.

As Bob Pattison remarked, in his notes on Stephen Leacock and his family, if even two Leacocks were together, life became fun. And so, even in those darkest days, when Uncle Stephen first took over the family responsibilities, he could always count on his mother to see the bright side of any situation and, like him, to joke about the little everyday mishaps.

He used his sense of humour as a shield for both of them – and together they shielded the little ones.

No, it was not all cloud, not even in the worst days. The Leacocks could always see the sunlight about to break, could always make one thin ray appear to fill the whole sky.

14

The Boy He Could Not Leave Behind Him

PART I – ENGLAND

My uncle had intended calling his last collection of writings *My Memories and What I Think*. However, he died before he got further than the early part of his life, so his publishers gave the book its present title, *The Boy I Left Behind Me*.

It is a good enough title, at first glance; but I do not think Uncle Stephen would have agreed to it. For he must have realized – though not likely quite so keenly as his family and friends – that he could never really leave behind him the boy who he had been.

For which fact we (his family), and the world can be thankful.

Intrigued by that boy who looked out, so often, from my uncle's eyes, who, time and again, slyly took over the professor's pen, I have, during these last few months, walked backward along the path that ended for Stephen Leacock in the small churchyard at Lake Simcoe, and found the boy Stephen's blaze-marks along the trail.

I travelled, in actual fact, to Hampshire, where Stephen Leacock began, one hundred years ago.

I went to the little house in Swanmore where he was born; and revisited Bury Lodge, where his mother had lived as a girl, and where the child Stephen was taken to visit.

I took the ferryboat to the Isle of Wight, where his father's people had lived, as well as his mother and his grandmother.

I stopped off in Portsmouth, and in Portchester, both vivid in my uncle's memory, although he was only six when he left Portchester.

I went to the little church at Soberton, where his mother had been born, and her father had preached; and to the church and high street of Hambledon, and to Hambledon Downs. If my uncle, later, did not actually recall these places (and I am sure that Granny, leaving for Canada, would have paid farewell visits to them), they were still part of that old, old Hampshire of which he later wrote so nostalgically.

The little house at Swanmore, (which is about eleven miles from Winchester), is, I was told by its present owners, Mr. and Mrs. Vincent Green, almost exactly as it was when my granny lived there. They bought it because they liked its antiquity, and except for making the necessary modern improvements in plumbing and heating, etc., they have left it almost unchanged. It is easy, then, to roll back time, and imagine that my grandmother and her three small children are still there.

The house, one of the old thatched cottages common to England at that time, was built several hundred years ago. I don't know how long Granny was there, or whether Uncle Dick, my second eldest uncle was born there. (Jim, the eldest, was born in South Africa.) At the most, I am pretty sure Granny was only there a year or two. In *The Boy I Left Behind Me* Uncle Stephen says, "During this period . . . my father and mother lived at different places . . . Swanmore and Shoreham, and then Portchester. Their large family . . . were born round this way, only two in the same place of the six born in England." (He slipped there, only *five* of the six children whom my grandparents brought out to Canada were born in England, the eldest, as I remarked earlier, having been born in South Africa.)

There were only three rooms downstairs in the cottage at Swanmore, unless you count the present kitchen, which was originally a pantry. There is the big old kitchen . . . a wonderful room, now the Green's living room . . . with a pitched ceiling, raftered and beamed with pitch-oak, an enormous bake oven, and a bread oven. There is a tiny little dining room, and a larger room behind it, originally a bedroom but now a study. Upstairs, there are two bedrooms, and two very small rooms which were apparently mere cubbyholes before the Greens came.

One of the upstairs bedrooms must have been my grandmother's and the other the children's nursery. (In true English style, the Leacock children slept in a common night nursery till they were practically in their teens; in Canada, at the farm, they also had a large day nursery – we would call it a playroom today. With the large Leacock family, the night nursery at the farm must have resembled one of the dormitories in which Lower School boys at a private school sleep.) The nursemaid doubtless occupied one of the cubbyholes in the Swanmore cottage, to be near the children; and the farmer and his wife who ran the place likely had the downstairs bedroom.

It is a very safe guess, then, that Stephen Leacock was born in one of the cosy little upstairs bedrooms. It would be hard to say which – they are about the same size, and each has its own small fireplace, and a low casement window overlooking the lawn and front garden.

The nursery and his mother's pretty bedroom were, then, the infant Stephen's first province. Nearby played his big brothers, and Nurse and Mother were comfortingly close. The big kitchen, too, was familiar, with its bustle and cheeriness, a bright blaze filling the huge fireplace, and reflecting from the pots and kettles.

From the low nursery window, and the safety of Nurse's or Mother's arms, the baby must have surveyed, for the first time, the outside world – the white flowering crown of the old tree, red roses nodding from long, swaying branches, the dark green of the cedar hedge encompassing the lighter green of the grass. In spring, through this same window, scents of garden and field would drift up to tease his young nostrils with their strange new freshness.

(Two modern houses have been built on what was then the property of the cottage, but you can still see the magnificent old flowering tree and a stretch of the hedge, as well as the remnants of the flower garden which was planted long before my grandmother's time.)

Born in winter, cold winds might blow about the house when the baby was small, but they were only a mild foretaste of the deep isolating snows of Canada. The nearby church was close enough that his mother could carry him there to be christened. She could walk with his brothers in the gently rolling fields behind the house, and point out to them, as they explored the copse, rabbits and squirrels, fronds of tall bracken, and small birds hopping about in the branches. She could still find the odd rose to clip from the tall rose tree near the brick wall; could teach the children "Robin, Robin Redbreast," as the plump, vermillion-breasted descendant of the old nursery rhyme hopped about the garden. And when spring came, they could search for primroses in the copse, for cuckoo-flowers and mayflowers.

This was the England Stephen Leacock remembered – a small, snug nursery, robins and roses, gently rolling fields, and a great, green hill where a game called cricket was played. Everything so safe and settled, for years and years before he was born, that it never entered anyone's mind that these things might change. It had all been there forever – it would be there till eternity. Or so it seemed then.

England was cosiness and comfort. It was the snug, thatched cottage at Swanmore; it was old, cream-walled Bury Lodge house, dozing over its fireplaces and its pink-walled garden, where fat bees murmured amongst the strawberries and sundial and fruit trees. It was a child, warm as a mouse over nursery tea, looking out upon a cold wind whipping the grey reaches of the ocean at Portchester. It was Grandfather Leacock's thick-walled house at Oak Hill, and many other old houses where want and discomfort had never been known.

England was pleasure and play – for children and grown-ups alike. It was sailing ships and sand-castles. It was cricket on the

Hambledon Downs, where most of the famous cricketers came to play, and the scores, recorded with a spidery pen, were pasted to the fire-screen in Great-Uncle Tom's house.

England was history. Charles II sleeping in Bury Lodge – the *original* Bury Lodge, that was now just a bit of wall in the garden. It was the Romans, whose coffins were found in the churchyards at Soberton, and at Portchester; Napoleon's soldiers, imprisoned in the castle; Nelson's ship, in Portsmouth harbour.

England was grey old Portchester, and Portchester castle, dreaming out over the sea. It was the church where, as the grown-up boy was later to write: "Uncle Charles preached quietly, so as not to wake the Normans, and the people gently dozed." It was Uncle Charles' vicarage, so close to the castle that a small boy could play in the keep (where cattle had once been herded during sieges) without his mother worrying. It was the subterranean passage to the castle dungeons. (His mother's sister, Aunt Cissy, had had nightmares as a child about the ghosts of prisoners whose bones had been found in these walls.)

England was the dead. The French prisoners and the English squires – cousins and connections so long gone that the inscriptions on their tombstones were nothing more than worn-down hieroglyphics on the moss-upholstered stones in the churchyard. And the ghost of Lord Nelson, surely, walking in the moonlight across the shattered decks of the *Victory*, as she bobbed at anchor across the Solent from Portchester.

England was ships and the sea. The *Victory*, and the big cargo ships at Portsmouth and Southampton. The great passenger sail-and-steamships. The little pleasure yachts, light and numerous as butterflies on the bright summer seas. And the tales of Papa's little blue yacht, upon which, long before Stephen and his brothers had been born, Papa and Mama, secretly engaged, used to meet at night while dear Uncle Charles thought her safely asleep in her bedroom.

England was the Isle of Wight, where his father had been born, and his mother had spent summers as a child; where Grandfather Leacock lived, and Stephen and his brothers were rarely allowed to visit because, as the boy wrote later, "he wanted the island for himself, and didn't want his sons to come crowding onto it. That's why they were sent out across the world wherever it was farthest." It was the Isle of Wight, whose sea-girt lands must have looked none the lovelier to the boys because it was forbidden. It was the house called "Oak Hill" on that island, where the stern old grandfather lived; a house with the panelled Georgian Hall, and with the pictures of ships and storms so numerous that a boy might wonder whether, in earlier days, the sea had never been calm about Wight. It was remembered visits to this house, one time in particular with Stephen, a small boy in a caped coat, in his mother's arms, and his brothers, Jim and Dick, also in caped coats, standing between their mother and their father to be photographed. (Everyone very solemn, except Grandfather's dog, as indeed the old man's unsmiling countenance would compel them to be.) The Isle of Wight, and other places they may never have visited, but which, through the years, they would come to know completely through their mother's realer-than-life descriptions – for instance, the children's great-grandmother's home, Westridge, which was not far from Oak Hill.

But before we go any further, let me tell you something about the origins of Stephen Leacock's family, and something of those events which led up to his parents' finally making that long journey across the sea – away from all the peace and safety they had known in England.

Let Uncle Stephen speak first. In *The Boy I Left Behind Me* he says:

> My family were Hampshire people on both sides. . . . The Leacocks lived on the Isle of Wight, where my grandfather had a house called Oak Hill near Ryde. . . . The Leacocks had made a lot of money out of plantations in Madiera and the Madiera wine trade, so much that my great-grandfather, John

Leacock, had retired and bought the house at Oak Hill. After that, nobody in the family did any work (any real work) for three generations, after which, in my generation, we were all broke and had to start work. . . . The senior member of the family got out a booklet about Madiera wines and the Leacock family and he put into it the . . . sentence: "The first recorded Leacock was a London day labourer, whose son was brought up at a charity school and went out as a ship's cabin boy to Madiera!"

My mother's family, the Butlers, were much better, though you couldn't really call them Hampshire people as they had not, at the time of which I speak, been in Hampshire for more than one hundred and fifty years. They lived, and still do, in a house called Bury Lodge, which is on a hill overlooking the immemorial village of Hambledon, Hants.

My grandfather (Stephen Leacock's father), Walter Peter Leacock was the second youngest son of Thomas Murdock Leacock, of Oak Hill, Isle of Wight. He was born there in 1848.

My grandmother, Agnes Emma Butler, was born in 1844 at Soberton, Hants. She was the youngest child of the Reverend Stephen Butler and Caroline Linton Palmer. Both her parents had been previously married and widowed, and each had had several children by these former marriages.

Peter's maternal grandmother, Mrs. Young, had been a close friend of Granny's mother, who had lived on the Isle of Wight; she and Granny's father, the Reverend Stephen Butler, were married there, in fact. Granny writes in her journal:

> The Youngs and Leacocks belonged to our church then. It was not till about that time that Mrs. (Thomas Murdock) Leacock and some of her sisters became Romanists; it was quite a grief to my father. . . . The Leacock boys John and Charlie (the two older sons of Thomas Murdock) used to go to school in Jersey, and the Channel Island boats came in to Southampton [where the Rev. Stephen Butler had the living

of Holy Trinity Church] late in the evening, so they stayed the night on their way to and from school for the holidays. Mrs. Leacock sometimes came over from the Island to meet the boys and stayed with us, too, once or twice. She brought Peter . . . he was not at school.

My mother told of one of these visits, when little Agnes' nurse discovered that the child had locked her toys in a cupboard, "because Peter Leacock breaks my toys." Mother could not forbear moralizing, "Little did she realize that much later Peter Leacock was to break something much more valuable than her toys . . . her heart."

There was then a period of quite a few years when these two children, Peter and Agnes, did not see one another. By the time they did meet again, Agnes was over ten, and her father, as well as her mother, had died.

Then, according to Granny's account, in June, 1866, when she was twenty-two and Peter eighteen, she went

> . . . to the Isle of Wight, with Uncle Charlie [the Reverend Charles Butler, her father's brother] to Seaview.
>
> One day we went to see the Leacocks . . . they were old friends of course, and I saw Peter then for the first time since we were children. He came over to Seaview every day and, late in the evening, when Uncle Charlie thought I had gone to my room I went out in Peter's boat with him. We were engaged before the summer was over, and married privately and later at All Saint's Church, Norfolk Street, London.

Granny writes also,

> That summer at Seaview, in 1866, when I was engaged to marry Peter, Lucy Patterson was with me. Uncle Charles took a cottage right on the beach at the end of the sea wall (I have a sketch of it somewhere) and it was just below there that Peter brought his blue boat. Sometimes there was another boy,

Stephen by name, with him, that was when Lucy was with me. We often spent the day at Oak Hill . . . and went to the Youngs at Westridge for croquet and stayed to dinner late in the evening.

I remember the sketch of Peter's "blue boat" that Granny refers to. It looked to be about thirty feet long, but what class it was one could not say from the small drawing. But I do know they both had a passion for sailing; and that my grandfather spent more time with his boat than with his books. Nor have I ever heard, from either the Leacocks or the Butlers, that he ever had any ambition to do anything else but sail, play cricket or croquet, and join in conversation with his friends.

Nor was there any reason why he should have to choose any other life. There was, as his son was later to remark, enough money that he did not need to work. Thomas Leacock had had his two older sons, John and Charlie, trained for the Navy, but he seems to have made no plans for either Peter or the youngest son, Edward (E. P. Leacock, the "Remarkable Uncle" of whom Stephen Leacock wrote in *Reader's Digest*). Peter was easygoing, witty and altogether charming, according to accounts of his family and of people in Canada who knew him when he was young. ("Peter? He was a fascinating man," replied my grandmother when, in my teens, I got up my courage to ask her about her husband. And, "one of the wittiest men I have ever met," said one of the Sibbald's, all of whom were close friends of the family.) If Peter's books bored him, and he deserted them to go sailing, I have never heard that anyone objected.

Although my great-grandfather's failure to educate his son has been obliquely criticised by both Uncle Stephen and the latter's biographers, I should like to offer in Great-grandfather's defence that his attitude was not unusual at that time, particularly in reference to the class to which the Leacocks and Butlers belonged. To care for one's own property (not a small business, when one considered the size of those properties, and the staff which was required to keep them going), to perhaps take part in local or larger politics, yes, even to sail, and to in general lead a full and happy life was not regarded as shiftless. It is only on this continent that the Puritan notion that every man must live by the sweat of his brow took root, and has eventually led to what seems to me the ridiculous inverse snobbery and smarminess of men of wealth going to great pains to pretend that work is an economic necessity to them. If the work they choose is, in fact, a fulfilment of their nature, and a genuine interest, well and good. But to spend one's life at uncongenial work, and very often not even to do very well at it, meanwhile depriving someone who *does* need the job – this notion, essentially North American, seems to me stupid.

At any rate, whatever his reasons may have been, Thomas Murdock allowed Peter to play his way through life until he was eighteen. But when he discovered that Peter was married, the party was over. Plans had already been made for the young man to go to the Colonies. Now they rapidly crystallized, and Thomas Leacock bought his son a cattle ranch in South Africa and shipped the young couple out there.

This venture failed. Ralph Curry says locusts ate the crops; I was told that the cattle died of a plague. Peter and Agnes, with their eldest child, Jim, who had been born in Africa, returned to England. My grandfather put them down in Hampshire, ". . . we were placed in Portchester," wrote Uncle Stephen ironically, "so that we couldn't get to the Isle of Wight, too often." In Swanmore (where Uncle Stephen was born), in Shoreham, Sussex, and Portchester and Liverpool, they spent almost ten years, with Peter ostensibly "educating" himself for farming by hobnobbing with the Hampshire farmers. According to my uncle, the schoolroom was usually the local tavern. During this interim period, Peter was bought another farm, in Kansas, but his young family never saw this place, as he returned in fairly short order, to report that grasshoppers had consumed the crops. It is hard to believe that the grasshoppers did not belong to the same fictitious category as the cattle plague (or Curry's locusts, whichever you will).

At any rate, upon his son's failure in Kansas old Thomas Leacock smartened up. He promptly purchased yet another farm for Peter, sent him ahead to get it ready for his family, then put Granny and the children (six of them, by this time) on the boat, with a one-way ticket to Canada. Peter did not return to his home in England until 1887, when he left the farm and his family for the last time. And my poor grandmother was there until 1891, when my mother had turned five and Uncle Stephen was finally able to move her out from under the mortgages and debts and general hopelessness of her situation on the farm. During that time, she had paid one visit to England to see the cousins who had been closer than sisters and brothers to her. That was to be the last time she saw her beloved homeland.

My great-grandfather sent his son a regular income, I believe, footed the bill for a private tutor for the boys and, when they were older, for Upper Canada College. But there was no question of their ever being allowed to return to England. It was exile, final and irrevocable.

PART II – CANADA

Stephen Leacock might, ostensibly, have left England behind him when, as a boy of six, he stepped aboard the *Sarmatian* – the three-masted sailing steamship which carried him with his family to Canada. But the truth of the matter was that he carried England with him, deeply buried inside his loyal and homesick heart.

There were so many things he took with him – things that, long, long years afterwards, were transplanted into his own life and inside his own home:

To play the game of cricket on a rough, mole-riddled field at Egypt, as well as later, when he was a young man, at Sutton and Orillia. Writes his friend Bob Pattison: "He played cricket in contests, with nearby towns; his flannels were quite enough to frighten any bowler into submission. And his socks were often a forerunner of what he later described in his 'A New Pathology,' notably 'Odditus Soccorum.' Necktie? What is a necktie when not necessary?"

To sail the small ships with the white wings on the broad blue waters of Lake Simcoe. Again, I quote Mr. Pattison.

> Lake Simcoe was his sailing course, he knew the shores well with all their tricks; there comes the remembrance one time when we were in a heavy wind close to Snake Island and he made the brag that he would sail close enough for me to throw a biscuit ashore there as he came about; and he did just that perfectly.
>
> There was one time, however, when he forgot the law of the sailor never to tie a rope when a slipknot would suffice. We had sailed from Beaverton towards Orillia in the *Pilot* yacht; he had taken off his shoes to change into a better, for was he not to make a social call which demanded the better pair? To facilitate such a change he had tied the boom-sheet to the centre-board handle just at the moment when a stiff breeze bore down on the Narrows. The good ship heeled till water, and plenty of it, rushed over the gunwale; the yacht was half-filled, and Stephen's shoes were entirely filled with Lake Simcoe's wetness. We rowed that boat the next mile which seemed like several miles, with what the natives call " a white ash breeze," meaning the use of oars of that variety of wood. The friends on shore cheered when we approached without glory, almost without shoes, and the story lost nothing of its worth when Stephen told it that evening; . . .
>
> We who were at his "Ship Breakfast," as he dubbed the affair, with the "table" to be set on the good ship *Pilot*, will recall that it was to be "at seven sharp." That breakfast bell rang at eleven, but it was the same morning anyway. The menu was to be fish caught right off the deck from the teeming waters of Lake Simcoe; Stephen had forgotten to notify the fish about this duty to his guests, so we tried bacon and eggs instead, and this turned out to be bread and butter prepared the night before, so as to be on the safe side. The oil stove was of uncertain date, so was the milk, called cream, which went with the coffee. N.B: There was no coffee!

Another unforgettable picture is of Stephen sitting on the rail of the excursion boat *Enterprise*; he had on an old shirt, rumpled flannels ("Inflatio Genu," to quote his "New Pathology" again) and worn tennis shoes. But soon he was dancing merrily as the steamer went up Barry Bay.

The good-natured yacht *Pilot* witnessed one night his application of physics. We were sailing from Barry in the Bay and darkness was at hand, when we saw a strange light in the distance. It was nothing but a lighted match he was holding against a tin cup as a reflector to notify us he was afloat over there. That night we slept, tried to, under a haycock on Big Bay Point, but not Stephen, he slept on the boards of the yacht as being softer than our earth-and-hay combination.

A place for gymnastics too. He gave us a sample of it when he started to climb the mast, and got half-way up, when the boat took its own manner of balancing, turned partly over, filled with water and spilled us all into the lake, the athlete along with us. He met such things with a laugh and his oft-repeated words, "And the last thing seen of the unfortunate sailors, they were clinging desperately to the torn rigging."

That same yacht was large enough to have a small boat attached. But not always. One of his brothers had rowed the small boat ashore and either utterly or purposely forgot that his dear brother Stephen was aboard the yacht and just might need the boat to get ashore himself. What was left, however, on the yacht were some airtight tanks, and a plank will do for a paddle under necessity; so he lashed some tanks together, and started shoreward in the tipsy craft; this was just at the time some of us arrived to see what would result; he was evidently proving that a curved line is the shortest distance between the ship and the shore, several curved lines in fact. . . .

That was not the only time he matched wits with his family, two of his brothers in particular. They were playing cards under deck, and refused to lend a hand of any kind in the heavy storm that was giving Stephen all he could do to keep that boat right side up. Only the sliding of the jackpot to the floor stopped the game and saved "Captain Leacock." The two were soon safely ashore, singing loudly a parody of a popular song of that day, "And the blow almost killed Stephen!"

To grow English roses and wallflowers and primroses and set a sundial in the garden of a white-walled house with a red-tile roof, even though it might never have the leaded panes he had remembered from England.

To sit decorously in another grey-walled stone church and listen to men of God, who preached in soft English accents lessons not very different from those he had listened to Great Uncle Charles preach. Again, Bob Pattison observes Uncle Stephen: "It was one Sunday in the Lake Shore Church . . . that during service we noticed his hand busily twisting that mop of hair which was always one of his physical possessions. One of his brothers endured that sight as long as possible, then whispered loud enough to be heard, 'Look at Stephen; he's trying to put a curl in it!' "

To lie at length in the churchyard of that same church . . . a churchyard with clipped cedars and crumbling tombstones and a grey stone wall, very like the churches at Portchester and Soberton, at Hambledon and Swanmore.

And from that small house in Swanmore, and from the Hampshire he knew as a child, where he first learned from his hard-pressed mother to meet despair with humour, Stephen Leacock carried that humour to use as a weapon for her defence, to shield them both from his own despair, to eventually give it to the world in page after page of mirth, in so great and unceasing a flood that one might think that wellspring had no bottom.

There were other things he learned, and carried with him always. From the men of his family, and from the gallant knights, whose names he spelled out from the tarnished old plates on the walls of Hampshire churches, and from the tombstones, he took two things: great bravery, and a sense of chivalry toward all women, and toward all who were weak or defenceless.

141

Here is another story which Mr. Pattison tells about him:

> ... that night of the violent storm, when his yatching party was storm-stayed on the sand islands near Georgina Island.... He left the party safe on the island, and sailed home through that fierce wind, wild and black, so as to get blankets and food for the women and children; a tough sail, but tougher had they spent that night without warmth and a meal.

Again, I quote Pattison: "A fair sample of his courtesy came out when some of us were returning from a garden-party at The Briars. He was mightily fond of tobacco and had taken his pipe from his pocket, but before lighting it, he asked permission of the ladies present. In this he included his sister by name."

I remember, too, an incident which embarrasses me very much to relate, but which was an instance of how Uncle Stephen's sense of courtesy never allowed him to slight even someone who might deserve it. My husband and I were having luncheon with him at the University Club, in Montreal, while we were on our honeymoon. The men were drinking ale with their meal, and he asked me if I would like some. For the past two weeks my husband had been initiating me into the life of the *bon vivant* – a role to which my rather puritanical mother had not accustomed me. The blood of my wine-importing Leacock forbears apparently ran in my veins, for it was immediately evident that I had a natural palate for the finest wines; nor had my husband, delighted to find so apt a pupil, stinted in his choice of wines when we ate. It had not been my business to note the cost of my favourites, and I did not. So when my uncle offered me an ale, I asked if I might not have wine instead. He took this in his stride, and asked if I had any favourite. I did, and named it, without realizing that my choice a very rare, and very expensive wine. My uncle said nothing, but his tone was rather dry as he instructed the steward to bring the bottle, only remarking, "I think perhaps you will find *one or two* bottles in the cellar." Years later, when I was doing the purchasing for my own house, and saw on the list "my wine" ... and its price ... my cheeks burned at my bad manners.

I must remark, too, that at this same luncheon my uncle again proved that his good manners were not reserved for "company," but accorded his family, too. He had, several years before, lent me $200 to help out with my university tuition. Small though this sum may appear now, I could not have gone to university without that help. The understanding was that I would pay him back when I was through and working; but I had, at the date of my marriage, (almost two years after my graduation) not only made no effort to do that, but had not, during all the time I was at University, written to him to tell him how I was getting along. It is true that when I did get a job, as an advertising copywriter, I already had massive doctor and dentist bills to pay, and a very small salary from which to pay them. Still, I should have, in all conscience, explained this to my uncle. When I was married, Uncle Stephen wired to say the $200 was his wedding present. I thanked him for this, of course, the day we had luncheon, and he brushed off my thanks. But later in the meal, when he and my husband were discussing the value of a university education he let fall an apparently careless aside, ". . . and, then, of course it is possible to go Rah! Rah! at college, and not bother about the books . . . isn't it, Betty?" Much later, when I was properly mature, I realized what a shabby way it had been for me to behave . . . and how tolerant Uncle Stephen had been not to reprove me.

It was at this luncheon, too, that my uncle tried, for the last time, to manipulate my destiny. He had already been told that, after the honeymoon, I intended going back to Toronto for another few months, to complete my work there; and had also heard that one reason for this was that I wanted to pay off all my debts before I embarked on my new life. I would join my husband on the R.C.A.F. station on Prince Edward Island when these two objectives had been realized. Uncle Stephen apparently had concluded that, by wiping out the debt I owed him, he had cleared the way to my going with Kim immediately; and when I still stuck by my guns and insisted that I could not walk out on an unfinished job like that, he pulled all the stops to persuade me against staying in Toronto. He reminded me, subtly, that a flyer's days might be numbered;

that patriotism implied my presence beside my husband; he delineated vividly the nobility of the role of warrior's wife compared to the shabbiness of "a little advertising job." I, on my side, could not make him realize that it was simply a question of fulfilling an obligation to which I had already committed myself. Finally my uncle gave up, with a good enough grace, considering how he had looked forward to our happiness in having our difficulties resolved. (I did not know whether or not to take as a compliment his closing remark, "Not like Daisy! I could play that woman like a violin. But not you!")

It was not, of course, ever a question of his simply wanting his own way. It was that he loved us all so . . . even an ungrateful niece whom he had not seen for several years. And, because of his love, he saw, so explicitly, in what direction our happiness lay.

These, then, were some of the aspects of the man called Stephen Leacock – and some of the childhood experiences which influenced and shaped his life.

But surely, you may ask at this point, the English boyhood ended when he was six. His experiences at the farm must have been more important than England.

Well, not more . . . but yes, very important, of course. So what about it . . . did Stephen Leacock leave the farm behind him when he moved away?

Some things he did leave, it is true, although not immediately. Let us say he sent back, and buried there, to the best of his ability, fear and bitterness and despair.

They were often with him throughout his later life, of course. Fear for his beloved wife, dying of cancer. The mounting fear that his son might never attain his full stature and health. Fear of poverty. Fear that his power to write and deliver might wane.

My Uncle Charlie told me once of times he had witnessed his brother as "a man tormented . . . a man of great despairs." But if this was true – and, if Uncle Charlie said so, it must have been true – although I make some allowance for Uncle Charlie's own extreme sensitivity to mood, which might exaggerate, still, Uncle

Stephen allowed very few people to witness his low moods. His son said, recently, "No, never depressed for long, always happy."

The bitterness? Yes, some of it was evident when he wrote about his grandfather Leacock; some small amount, too, against his older brothers, Jim and Dick. One can read between the lines of *The Boy I Left Behind Me* – Stephen perhaps felt that they moved out a little too easily from the family responsibilities which he was left to shoulder.

Yet toward the man against whom one might have expected Stephen Leacock to feel the greatest bitterness – his father – he was surprisingly tolerant. It is true that he was never able to bring himself to see him again. Nevertheless, in his writing, and in private references, he tried to joke about him, he tried to understand; and this must have been very hard indeed for the boy who saw his beloved mother and his little brothers and sisters suffer at the drunkard's hands.

Yes, he left behind him at the farm most of the bad things ... the bitterness, fear and despair. But he took with him most of the boy who had lived there from the age of six till he left, at twelve, to go to Upper Canada College.

My mother wrote of "the host of memories of those days (at the farm) when his humour was mingled with those younger brothers and sisters. Humour shared with Mother to brighten up her days, as, far from her beloved England, she rose above discouragement and loneliness." She went on to say:

> I don't remember Stephen being at the farm much in the summer, although he spent most of the holidays there. But in the winter, and especially at Christmas, I remember very clearly, he used to bring Dot and me wonderful toys "from town" (Toronto). He loved Christmas, and in later years he would have us hang up pillow slips instead of stockings. "Stockings aren't half big enough," he'd say. If the pillow slips were only half full we never noticed. It was the excitement, Christmas morning, of diving into them to see what we'd get.

I do remember one Christmas at the farm. Dot was six and I was four. Stephen got Dot skates and after breakfast we went down to the pond. (Our farm was inland, away from either Lake Simcoe or the Black River.) Stephen took a kitchen chair and had Dot push it about to learn to skate, which she did in no time at all. Every Christmas we got new hand sleighs, and we would try them out as soon as we were dressed, and while we lived on the farm we would go sleigh-riding across the south fields which sloped away from the house.

Of these hand sleighs, which "Santa Claus" Stephen gave his little sisters, Mother also relates: "Stephen and the boys always borrowed them and made them into an ice-boat by putting a long board between them and hoisting a sail. We used to stand on the shore and watch the boys sailing away toward the Indian (Georgina) Island!" (On these occasions it is obvious that the Leacocks must have made the trip down to the lake for the ice-boating.) "We thought all 'the boys' were wonderful, and never questioned the rightness of having our sleighs confiscated, as long as they were returned intact when the holidays were over."

Mother also remarked, "To be 'the baby' had its disadvantages. The 'little boys,' as my ten- and twelve-year-old brothers, George and Teddy were called, teased me unmercifully; even the 'big boys' (Jim, Dick, Stephen and Charlie) sometimes took a hand, hanging my doll up in an apple tree, etc. . . ."

Bob Pattison recalled how Uncle Stephen "used to mimic one of his small sisters, who had then a rather squeaky voice . . . to her own delight." This, I know, was Aunt Dot; Stephen, too, invented for her, because of the sprinkling of fine freckles on her thin, white face, the nickname "Turkey-Egg."

This thoroughly normal youngster was the same stern responsible youth who, some years before, had taken over the family cares when he sent his father away. Even though Mother might suffer momentarily it is easy to see why she should adore him and say, as she once did, "he was better than any father could have been." Yes, . . . young, handsome, full of fun . . . this was the boy who, gratefully for us all, Stephen Leacock never did leave behind him."

There were other bits and wisps I remember Mother telling me of her big brother. Of the times he used to have her mother put her and Dot on the train and send them up to Toronto, where he would meet them and take them to the theatre, and show them "the sights." As Mother remarked, too, in those years his sisters were rather shabby little bumpkins, and it must have cost their brother, a young master at Upper Canada, quite an effort to introduce them to his smart fellow collegians.

Yet he gave the little sisters those treats, and my mother used to tell me of how very glamorous he and his college friends used to appear to them. One incident which made a lasting impression with her was of a "stag" dinner party he gave, at his current boarding house, for some of his friends. After one particulary sacred toast the young blades flung their wine glasses over their shoulders, shattering them so that they might not be defiled by toasting lesser persons. . . . Whereupon the landlady appeared, dressing them down soundly as if they were naughty little boys. Apparently she did not appreciate the sophistication of boarder Leacock! (I do not know whether the little girls were present to witness Stephen's humiliation, but Mother described it so graphically that I think they must have been allowed downstairs for at least a part of the dinner.)

Mother once read me a letter her big brother wrote in reply to her request that he send her a play for her school Christmas concert. I cannot recall the exact words, but they were very much to this effect: "A play for your concert? Yes, my pet, you shall have it. And what shall it be . . . ?" going on to suggest themes for her acceptance.

Mother told me, too, of Uncle Stephen taking Granny to the theatre one evening, and bringing her a corsage of violets for the occasion. His son lately told me that his father had confessed to him that he was, when young, often embarrassed by his mother's shabbiness. And so he may have been on this occasion. But whatever twinges of shame he might have felt, they must have been erased when, holding the flowers against her worn furs, Granny smiled at her own reflection in the mirror. "Oh, my, I really do look someone," she murmured.

I thought of this story when, in December, 1969, I stood in the house at Brighton where Granny, as a girl, used to visit her cousin George Butler at Easter. She wrote, "He used to have me down to late dinner before I was 'out' and had parties on purpose for me." I looked about me at the beautiful drawing room, with its decorated ceiling and fireplace, its crystal chandelier and its big windows overlooking the sea. I thought of the gracious life she had known at this house in Brighton, and of the fêtes at the barracks of the Third Hussars at Hamilton which she and her cousin Tom Butler used to go to when she was older; of the yatching parties at the Isle of Wight; of the pleasures and gaieties of that lost life, when pretty clothes and corsages came as a matter of course. And I imagine that something like these thoughts must have been in my uncle's mind too; that a theatre ticket and a small bunch of violets were a token of his understanding of what it must have meant to Granny to have been deprived all those years of even a small taste of a more gracious life.

All my mother's brothers were generous and kind-hearted; but with some of them it was often "out of sight, out of mind." It was never so with Uncle Stephen. When he assumed the father's responsibilities, he also felt it his obligation to provide all the treats and graces a kind father might lavish on his children. Nor did he ever outgrow these qualities of generosity and thoughtfulness.

No, Stephen Leacock never did leave behind him the boy who he had been.

15

You, too, can Bake a Cake Like Stephen Leacock's Mother Used to Make

Stephen Leacock might have lived and died an anonymous — and contented — farmer, had not his mother been so atrocious a cook. As it was, he fled the parental farm at an early age, a fugitive from cannonball puddings and burned beef.

He subsequently authored over sixty books. It is true that in none of them (not even in his autobiography, *The Boy I Left Behind Me*) does Leacock mention the *cuisine* at the farm. This may have been due to a natural distaste for displaying his sufferings in public; or it may have been simply because he was a gallant man, who also worshipped his mother. But the horrors of Agnes Butler Leacock's table were often the subject of reminiscence when her children were together. This I know, because I often eavesdropped on such conversations among the grown-ups.

Nor did any of their tales amaze me. For quite how awful Granny's cooking could be I knew first hand, not only because I was an annual summer guest in her home, but because our household had inherited her culinary convention. My mother, Daisy, was fiercely loyal to *her* mother, and she would never have dreamed of going back upon her childhood indoctrinations. Indeed, I never recall Mother referring to, let alone owning, any cookbook but the tattered scribbler in which she had copied her parent's "Receipts" (I believe this to have been a mis-spelling of Recipes, for my mother was a chronically and unashamedly poor speller).

I wish I had preserved Mother's Receipt Book, because I might have allowed the interested reader to have, quite literally, tasted its contents. My mother was swift, but sloppy, when she cooked, and often a large blob of dough or a raisin or some equally adhesive ingredient spattered from her mixing spoon and descended to the page. Dried with time, and pressed flat between the leaves, these dehydrated scraps vividly recall the picture of Daisy, lips tightly set against her task, the large, old, chipped ironstone mixing bowl braced against her hip, and the wooden mixing spoon firmly grasped in her small floury hand, as she gave the lumpy mixture the twenty-odd lightning turns which were her interpretation of "mix thoroughly." Not only did spoon and bowl drip, but Daisy herself was usually elbow-deep in either mix or flour.

The fare produced by benefit of the Receipt Book was heavy rather than hearty. In fact, my brothers, my sister and I frequently found ourselves almost weighted to our chairs due to our vast intake of starch, suet and flour. I recall my childhood as passed in a sort of grey torpor. My mother explained my lethargy by labelling me a bookworm, but in view of the physical energy I suddenly generated after I left home, I think the reading was more effect than cause. Physically incapable of moving further than the couch in the playroom, I read groggily until the bell summoned me to yet another glutting of my stomach with Spotted Dogs, white sauces and dumplings.

I never knew my grandmother to personally prepare so much as a cup of tea, but as my Uncle George once said, she liked to give the impression that she cooked. "She comes to the door wiping her hands on her apron," he remarked, "but I have an idea that when she hears visitors coming she runs to the kitchen and dips her hands into the bag of flour." When I was a child, Granny always had domestic staff: a housekeeper, and a little maid from the village. On the farm, of course, she had had "hired help," but perhaps she did lend a hand in the kitchen when her children were small. At any rate, she certainly made sure that all her maids were properly trained in the Leacock *cuisine*.

This school of cooking was so rare that, in a lifetime, I have never since tasted so much as one dish which duplicated, in anything but name, the fare upon which I and my siblings and many of our cousins were reared. It is difficult to find an adjective which will give you an idea of the special character of Granny's cooking. "Inedible" or indigestible" is obviously untrue, since all eleven of Agnes Leacock's children grew to exceptionally vigorous maturity. "Awful" or just plain "bad" implies failure ... and in no single respect could one have accused this dauntless, fiercely intelligent little person of failure. If, in fact, the results of her culinary endeavours did not match those of housewives commonly considered successful, it was due to an excess of creativity rather than to a lack of talent. Everything my grandmother undertook bore the mark of her strong individualism. The original creator of the Apple Dumplings and Gooseberry Fools which I encountered at my mother's table was a fit parent for the author of *Moonbeams from the Larger Lunacy* and *Sunshine Sketches of a Little Town*.

My sister and I once tried to figure out the origin of this distinctive brand of cooking. We were certain that Granny had not been taught to cook as a girl. She rode well, and taught her sons cricket, but the only maidenly accomplishments I ever heard claimed for her were piano playing and sketching. Her first encounter with full-scale domesticity must have come when she and my grandfather were shipped off to that cattle ranch in the Transvaal, where, I am quite sure, no English ranch-owner's wife ever did anything so menial as cook.

But stay! What about that mysterious plague which struck the cattle, causing them all to die? Could it be that the young bride had already embarked upon those culinary adventures whose fruits were to later colour with awe the reminiscences of her descendants? Could it be that Granny, not yet sufficiently confident of her skill to offer the products of her labour to her groom, tried them out on the cattle? Was the "plague" actually one of her early baking failures?

Realizing that her education in cooking must have been, at best, skimpy, Margaret and I tried to visualize how Granny would have undertaken the task of instructing her small staff into the niceties of an English gentleman's table.

The cooking of her Canadian neighbours was, of course, quite out of the question for the table of an English gentleman and his family. This may sound odd, but unless you have been reared, as I was, a second-generation Canadian of Anglo-Saxon descent, I do not believe you can appreciate the strength of the British caste system, when transplanted to this soil. As far as Granny was concerned, the fact that her children should have to go to school with "common children" was bad enough; that they should adopt Canadian habits was unthinkable – in cuisine, as well as in costume.

Equal in importance in upholding caste was the necessity of remaining English. When I was a child, in spite of the fact that my mother and all four of her children had been born in Canada, "home" was England. We were cautioned against speaking like Canadians, who were guilty, we were asked to observe, of such verbal *gaucheries* as "ornj," "furst," and "winder"; the correct (i.e. English) pronunciations for "orange," "forest," and "window" being, of course, "Ah-rahnj," "fah-rest," and "win-dough." The result of this diligent policing of our speech was that we grew up with such an exquisitely rare accent that to this day I am sometimes asked what school I attended, my interrogater being under the impression that I must have acquired my education in some small, incredibly select private school.

In other areas, too, (manners, dress, even thought) we were carefully taught to eschew all things Canadian. We were, in fact, brought up under the impression that we were only passing through Canada. A rather long stay, perhaps, but eventually we would go home – to England.

So no matter how accomplished the novice in the Leacock kitchen might be in satisfying the appetites of the robust farmhands who sat at her mother's table, no matter how plump and pink-cheeked she might present herself, the product of similar fare, the hireling domestic must begin all over again and learn to cook the English way – or at least Granny's interpretation of it.

I think I have some insight into Granny's probable approach to learning the art. I deduced it from the common impression shared by all her descendants. When faced with one of her dishes, one's immediate reaction was of something left out, of something gone awry. How else to explain the inside-outness, the upside-downness? The common denominator of all the dishes we were offered was that they always appeared to be the opposite of the orthodox version. Granny's cakes, for instance, attained the perfect silhouette . . . *in reverse*. Whereas common Canadian cooks produced cakes that rose to the edges of the pan, and soared loftily in the centre, ours attained a maximum height about a quarter of the way up the sides, than sank into a deep depression in the middle. Whereas other puddings and breads were golden and crusty outside and delectably tender within, ours were gluey and pale outside and hard as seamen's biscuit inside. Whilst ordinary cooks' gravies were rich brown and uniformly thick, ours were pale fawn, with thick lumps beneath a thin liquid.

I think my grandmother must simply have cast back nostalgically for the names of her favourite childhood dishes, then tried to deduce how they had been made, rather as she would have tackled a problem in algebra, at which, I have been told, she had been very good. She likely began with certain known quantities. "Milk Pudding *must* have milk in it," I can imagine her saying to herself, ". . . and, let me see, it *tasted* like vanilla; yes, I think a bit of vanilla." Then she must have tried out a few unknowns, the X's of the formula. "Flour thickens things, I *think* . . . or is it cornstarch? . . . and milk pudding is thick. Let's put in some flour." The resulting "Solution" or answer to the problem passed for a "Receipt," and was handed on to the maid to put into practice. That all Granny's recipes were written by hand, and that her handwriting was so nearly illegible that her letters were used as puzzles by us when we were teen-agers, could not have made the girl's work any easier.

Quantities must have been arrived at by calculating the size of the desired end-result, which allowed a rough proportioning of the ingredients. Whatever the amounts given, they were a mere formality, if I can judge by watching my mother making up one of Granny's recipes. Flour and sugar were generally "measured," either by shaking the bag over the mixing bowl several times, or by the fistful. Occasionally a cup was employed; not a measuring cup, just any old cup. Sometimes mother banged the cup briskly on the table, sometimes she didn't; this seemed to depend upon her mood rather than upon the recipe. That this banging might make a difference of as much as half a cup of flour or sugar would not have disturbed her. I can still recall her scorn when I attended Domestic Science classes and she found me *sifting* the flour into a cup – and a measuring cup at that!

Method? How could my little grandmother have known how to combine all these guessed-at ingredients to create the desired Spotted Dog, Roly-Poly or Toad-in-the-Hole? The answer is she couldn't – so she guessed. There is no other explanation for the wild divergence of her recipes from the conventional versions.

There was, however, a certain brave grandeur to her directions. There was none of this namby-pamby breaking eggs into a saucer before separating whites from yolks, as I was instructed at cooking school, or "beat until stiff but not dry." "Separate the eggs (from each other, perhaps?), and beat till stiff," she ordered briskly. "Put in enough raisins" (or currants, candy peel, etc.) was another instruction that saved time and the washing of a measuring cup. "Enough? Why, enough for everyone in the family, you dimwitted girl! Enough means enough!" Again, "Mix ingredients and roll," reads the succinct how-to of baking pie crust.

Let me describe for you a few of the family specialities. There were tarts and turnovers, usually fruit. (Canadians called these "pies" and filled them with such "common" ingredients as banana cream, raisins and chocolate custard.) "Why is it," my Uncle George marvelled, driving away from Sutton after a Sunday dinner, "that one can never eat the filling *and* the crust of Mother's pies?"

My own mother's pies had one advantage over those served at Bury Lodge. One could not depend upon the filling, it is true; but one knew better than to *ever* attempt to eat the crust. In fact, as most of our away-from-home meals were birthday parties, where cake rather than pie was the dessert, we were adults and out in the world before we knew that pie-crusts *could* be eaten. We thought they were like the cardboard plates used in those days by commercial bakers – just a means of containing the dessert. As a matter of fact, cardboard would have been delectably tender compared to Mother's pie crust. It had a close affinity to concrete – and concrete mixed by an unscrupulous contractor, at that. Her "shells" were riddled with craters and fissures, beneath which driblets of filling would hide themselves, forever safe from greedy fork or spoon. "Mix well and roll," the recipe had said. Perhaps "roll" referred to the finished product. Maybe these discs (which came, incidentally, in just two shades, off-white and very dark brown) were originally intended as playthings for the infant Leacocks, like hoops or wagon-wheels.

I have implied that my mother's pie fillings were sometimes good. The adjective is relative. They were sometimes good compared to the crusts. That is, one sometimes, though rarely, found a few slices of apple, a spoonful of raspberries or cherries, which were sufficiently cooked to be eaten without caution; one occasionally discovered a small quantity of fruit juice which had run away from the corn starch with which all fillings were thickened. But as a general rule fillings were either undercooked or overcooked. By undercooked I mean they gave one the impression that Mother had forgotten to insert the filling till after the crust had been baked. How she accomplished this, considering the strength of the finished crust, I do not know. But how else could she have burned the crust black while inside were completely raw chips of apple? Overcooked, on the other hand, means that the so-called fruit was reduced to a thin, brittle slab of black whose fruit origin had to be taken on faith. "I thought you liked apple pie, dear," Mother would remark in disappointment, as the diner pushed his plate away; and thus he would discover the exact nature of the offering.

English suet puddings, too, were stand-bys on our menus. At their best, I find this type of dessert too heavy for my taste, but I have eaten them as a guest of English friends of my mother, and they were miracles of levity compared to those served at our table. Steamed puddings à la Leacock were shrunken, leaden shapes, frightfully blistered, sweating and sickly outside, stiffly packed on the inside. A steam pudding was grandly presented on a platter, the sauce being served in a separate dish.

Mother made just two types of pudding sauce: the one thin as water, the other as thick as the white paste we were given for our scrapbooks. Both were gluey, and filled with lumps which dissolved into uncooked flour beneath the tooth of the unwary. All Leacock trenchermen consumed uncooked flour as a matter of course. It surrounded currants and fruit in cakes and steamed puddings; it hid beneath pastry shells and squirted out like powder when one's fork cut through a bump; it floated, like an uncooked dumpling, in gravy. Sugar, which in my childhood was much coarser than nowadays, also managed to preserve itself in raw lumps throughout cakes and puddings; it was particularly perilous to bite into a lump of brown sugar, since the lid of the ancient tin in which it was kept did not fit properly, and the sugar formed into very hard lumps, sometimes the size of a pigeon's egg.

I do not know how things went when my aunts and uncles and mother were little, but I know that in our family desserts were not often eaten. I do not mean that they were not presented on the menu. I simply mean that we did not eat them. We knew what was expected of us, so, in spite of almost daily disillusionment, we *tried* to eat them, but usually the major part of the dish defied penetration by fork or spoon; and what was, literally, possible to eat generally profoundly discouraged the palate after the first few mouthfuls. (Except, that is, for those times which each of us will never forget, when we suddenly bit into the dessert's total allotment of spice or flavouring – an inevitable risk when one considered the few hasty turns with the wooden spoon that passed for mixing in our kitchen. Unless you have taken into your mouth a spoonful of uncooked, powdered ginger, or a puddle of full-strength vanilla, I do not think you can realize the robustness of our optimism, or the firmness of my mother's discipline, in continuing to broach her desserts.)

In fact, since it was the usual rule for a pudding to return to the kitchen almost the same size as it was presented by the maid, I have often wondered why my mother bothered to prepare a dessert at all. It might have been more to the point to present us each with a token or a certificate declaring that we had had our dessert.

You may, perhaps, wonder if there were not complaints from those who were expected to eat the foods I have described. You do not realize the awe in which my grandmother was held by her offspring. My mother, on the other hand, did not depend entirely upon maternal respect. We were reared with two major precepts, which were such effective prohibitions that they were not even discussed among the four of us till after we had grown up. These rules were: (1) Never talk about money; and (2) Do not discuss your food.

I can understand now that these were not merely social taboos with my mother, but desperately necessary measures of self-defence. We had no money, which discovery might have frightened small children; and had we been allowed to discuss our food, we might have staged an open mutiny. As it was, although each of sometimes entertained ugly suspicions on each score, deprived of the opportunity to compare notes with our siblings, we cast them out as shameful and ungrateful.

We came closest to rebelling against the rigours of our board after we had attended a birthday party or a meal at a playmate's home. There we feasted on cakes as high as band-boxes, which hid their feathery deliciousness beneath three-inch overcoats of rich, swirly, boiled frosting. Lucky guests picked dimes and quarters from these confections as prizes. (Our birthday cakes were hard, sunken in the centre, mined with uncooked fruit, and insufficiently concealed beneath a thin, runny "icing" of water and icing sugar in which one could plainly see a few meagre lumps of uncreamed butter; and there was never more than a nickel in any of them.) At these foreign tables we also encountered ice-cream served with chocolate or butterscotch sauce, and such marvels as angel cakes, triple-layer cakes, marble cakes, and, wonder of wonders, strawberry shortcake. Sandwiches held tuna fish, minced chicken and similar *gourmet* fillings; and, too, the crusts had been cut off. Canada Dry, olives and gherkins, and after-dinner mints were other refinements of our playmates' feasts. (Our sandwiches were inevitably egg or peanut butter. Raspberry vinegar, a home-made libation whose sharpness was most unkind to unaccustomed throats, was served in summer; pallid cocoa, with lumps of undissolved cocoa was, of course, offered in winter.)

Dreams of a world in which such fine fare might be one's daily lot sometimes moved the young guest, returning to the home table, to mention these delicacies to our mother. I do not remember how Mother managed to preserve the rules of hospitality, and at the same time discourage such dangerous comparisons, but I know that all of us, rather than envying our playmates, ended by looking down upon their feasts as "common" and "Canadian." To this day, when I am served an especially fluffy cake or rich pie – particularly such vulgar Colonialisms as strawberry shortcake or coconut cream pie – I instinctively find myself thinking, "Poor woman . . . but after all, what can one expect of a Canadian?"

Quite likely, I shall say to my son, the next time he comes for dinner, "But I thought you *liked* rhubarb pie, dear . . . " and he will look up, enlightened, from the brown-and-black wedge on his plate.

The Leacock *cuisine* dies hard.

16

A Funeral at the Lake

There can be no question about it, Uncle Stephen's funeral was not the success it should have been. Perhaps because he spoiled everything by choosing an expensive, show-off box, and getting himself cremated; or maybe it was because he timed his demise so badly.

Through the years, we had worked out a pretty good drill for funerals in the Leacock family. We had a fifty-buck box, done up in the favourite colour of the incumbent; we had the places ready at Sibbald's Church, under the Upside-Down Tree; there was still plenty of room to scribble another name on Granny's stone cross; and Harve Taylor, the Sutton undertaker, could have buried any Leacock in his sleep, so used was he to doing it.

So you see, in a way, Uncle Stephen, when he died, should have been no trouble at all to anybody. But the way things turned out, it was trouble, trouble from start to finish.

Perhaps I should tell you a bit about the traditional Leacock family funeral, before I go on to Uncle Stephen's fiasco.

It seems to me it was Granny herself who set the fashion for the fifty-buck box. (We called it that not through delicacy, but as a matter of convenience.) I think my grandmother must have discussed the question, either in a general way, or explicitly, with her own burial in mind, with Mr. Taylor, for I recall being told of her comments when she heard how much she could anticipate paying. The price, I am sure, to those who have shopped around for funerary furnishings, was modest by contemporary standards, but Granny was outraged. "Nonsense!" she is reported to have exclaimed. "There is no need to throw away money like that! Taylor must have something plainer." I should point out that my grandmother's objections were by no means primarily dictated by economy; she felt, as we all do, that emphasis on the physical trappings of burial was all wrong. It was not the body which was important, but the soul which had fled it. The interment of the empty body was the least important part of the religious ceremony which marked the passing of the spirit.

When the time came for Granny's burial, no one, of course, would have dared go against her wishes. So, at the family's insistence, and, I am sure, against his own convictions, Harve Taylor came up with a box which might have been designed by Granny herself. It was a plain pine box, with inexpensive metal handles . . . such as one might, I imagine, use for the burial of a pauper. It was covered with cloth . . . a touch conceived by Mr. Taylor himself, perhaps more as a sop to his professional pride and own sense of what was fitting, than to ours. As it turned out, that cloth covering so pleased us that from then on Harve didn't have a chance of selling any of us anything but the fifty-buck box.

The cloth could be had, it turned out, in different colours; and much of the bereaved family's grief at the passing of one of their members was mitigated by their absorption in the choice of the appropriate colour. Granny's coffin (please do not ask me to say "casket" – to me a casket is one of those boxes pirates dig out of the sand, with Pieces of Eight and ropes of pearls spilling out of it). Granny's coffin, as I was about to say, was covered with a lavender-coloured material, in much the same shade as she used to choose for her morning dresses and the puff-sleeved, knickered swimming suits which the village dressmaker ran up for her. Aunt Dot chose – or had chosen for her – a deep Persian blue, in a tasteful jacquard weave. Aunt Maymee had a deep blue, too, as I remember.

Granted that the price of coffins is, on the whole, outrageously out of proportion to the quality of material or workmanship put into them, I imagine that even in those far-off thirties or forties, when Harve Taylor devised the box which he sold us for fifty dollars, he was losing money. And he continued to lose on the deal, for the price once set, the family regarded it as permanent. Taylor found himself in the same fix as poor Jack Sibbald. As you may recall, at the beginning of Granny's twenty-odd-year tenancy of the lakeshore cottage, he had set a price that was low even for the times, only to find that, in his tenant's eyes, he had fixed it forever. So Taylor, too, found himself expected to continue to turn out Leacock coffins at fifty dollars apiece. As he boxed some four to six Leacocks, he must have groaned with more than sympathy at the passing of a friend each time he picked up the phone to hear the news that another Leacock was "coming up to the church," as the phrase went.

The rest of the funeral routine became very smooth, with practice, the box having been decided upon in advance, and the plot often pre-decided, too. (If some member of the family had already broken ground, so to speak, their mate was naturally buried beside them – or, in one case, in with them. For example, Uncle Henry Bergh had been cremated, and the grave-digger thriftily cut a neat square foot of earth out of Aunt Maymee's grave, within which were placed her husband's ashes.) The organist presented no problem, since he was already familiar with the deceased one's favourite hymns, and the guest-list, of course, was always basically the same. So there really wasn't much more to do except notify Harve of the event, and to choose the colour of the coffin covering.

The office of Master of Ceremonies, as it were, automatically fell to the oldest surviving member of the family, provided they lived near enough to Sutton for this to be practical. I found myself officiating at Uncle Charlie's funeral – and really, with the drill so well worked out through the years, and thanks to having had so many previous opportunities to observe the necessary manoeuvres, it was practically no trouble at all.

Early in the history of our family burials, things had not always been so smooth. Take Uncle Dick's and Uncle Jim's burial, for instance. Uncle Dick, the second son, died before his elder brother Jim. ("Oh, not one of the little boys!" Granny is said to have protested when they came to break the news to her. She was apparently relieved to hear it was one of the "big boys" – doubtless feeling that they were mature enough to stand up to death; whereas George and Teddy, the "little boys," being mere striplings in their early fifties, were obviously too tender for such blows.)

Dick was buried in the States (Yonkers, I believe), where his widow, Aunt Kate, had wanted him to be, so that she might pay frequent visits to his grave. However, apparently uneasy at his presumptuousness in preceding his older brother, he, literally, could not rest in peace. Some time after his interment in Yonkers he erupted from the grave and had to be re-buried. An exploding gas main was the ostensible reason for his rising again from the dead; but I think it more likely that he left the uncongenial soil under his own volition. At any rate, since Kate would not object, as she was dead by then, and thus able to walk hand in hand with Uncle Dick in fields more beautiful than those of the Yonkers cemetery, Granny welcomed him home to Sutton. Uncle Charlie and "Little Charlie" (my grown cousin Charlie Sheppard) brought what remained of his remains back to the lakeshore churchyard. With him came Uncle Jim, who had rather inconveniently died of pneumonia.

This indecision on Uncle Dick's part, and Uncle Jim's last-minute whim to tag along with him, made it hard going for Uncle Charlie, as I am sure you can appreciate. But at least it got the family into the habit of funerals, and by the time that Uncle Stephen died, the routine should have been as smooth as silk.

The head of the family, then, had only to phone Harve Taylor to set the wheels in motion. The conversation was pretty stereotyped: "Harve, Maymee's gone," it would begin. There would then ensue a brief conversation regarding the nature of the deceased one's passing – from what affliction (old age, of course, was not regarded as a legitimate excuse for leaving the family party), details of the last hours, etc. This bit of politeness out of the way, the two got down to business. "When will you be bringing her up, George?" Harve would enquire. This noted, the two would work out a list of pallbearers, comfortable in the knowledge that if any of those chosen from abroad (Toronto, Belleville, Calgary) should decline the honour or default at the last minute, Harve could easily substitute from a standing list of family friends in Sutton. Family flowers too were often left to Taylor, who knew each Leacock's favourite bloom.

There then remained only the final decision about the location of the plot (an easy one, as I have noted), before they settled down to the most important detail of the funeral, the all-important choice of colour for the material which would cover the box. "Blue, I think, Harve," Uncle George might suggest. "Maymee was always partial to blue." Then Harve would describe a bit of material he happened to have handy in just the right shade of blue. "Sounds great, Harve," Uncle George would agree, and then ring off with "See you Tuesday at three, then," or whatever day and time they had decided upon.

I have often thought how tempted Mr. Taylor must have been, considering the fact that he could have got nothing but a possible income-tax exemption out of a Leacock funeral, to fob us off with a leftover end of cloth. But we were always pleased with the covering; and, for that matter, would likely have raised a great rumpus if we had thought the person who was, so to speak, wearing it, would not have liked it. Taylor could have put a cardboard bottom in the coffin, fastened it together with staples or Scotch tape, given it rope handles and a gimcrack catch, and no one would have noticed; but the cloth must be right. It was the covering that "made" the fifty-buck box.

As to our plot, it is just to the west of Sibbald's Church, which, as I remarked earlier, is on the shores of Lake Simcoe. The plot lies almost directly below the big stained glass window at the rear of St. George's Church (the proper name for Sibbald's Church), and is very easy to find, because of the Upside-Down Tree.

There has been in the family, and among outsiders too, much discussion of what the correct name is for the Upside-Down Tree. Some people call it an umbrella tree; others a monkey tree, and some say that it is planted upside down, with what appear to be its branches actually being its roots. What the reason for this whimsy might be, I have no idea.

Perhaps you would like to go up to Lake Simcoe and see this tree for yourself. We'll be glad to welcome you, but you'd better plan to visit us soon – some of the branches of the Upside-Down Tree are getting so heavy that they may break off any year now.

At any rate, there we all are, beneath the spreading boughs (or roots, whichever you will), with plenty of room for all, thanks to Uncle George's foresight. "By Jove, we're running out of space," he ejaculated, turning from my father's still-open grave. Then he took a rapid census of future tenants of the Leacock plot:

"Stephen? Dickie? Margie? Harry? Betty? Do you all want to come?" he demanded. I accepted with alacrity, eager to make sure of the last bit of land I am ever likely to own. (I resisted the impulse to add, "I don't know exactly *when* I'll be coming, but I'll let you know later.")

The others were equally anxious to be assured of their rightful places.

"Then we'd better do something about it soon," said Uncle George.

He was as good as his word. By the following week he informed us that he had bought more land on the other side of the tree and that there was now "plenty of room for all."

Other families in Sibbald's Churchyard lie beneath neatly clipped cedars and yew trees. Many of them have rose-bushes or other pretties growing from their remains; or are content with the conventional decency of a granite shaft or cross. The Sibbalds themselves have a little private yard, enclosed by cedars, with several neat chain fences to ensure the privacy of the less sociable members of the family. Many of the churchyard's tenants have these little fences, a bit of quiet tastefulness which, as a child, I often coveted for my relatives; it was also a cruel blow when I discovered that Granny had specified that only her name and the pertinent statistics were to be cut in her stone; the Sibbald's coat of arms, cut into one of their ancestor's stones, had long been a thorn in my flesh, which I had sustained by dreaming of the day when one of us should be sufficiently rich and important to display the Leacock rooster on his or her tombstone.

The grass on almost all the other graves is neatly clipped, and smooth and green as a freshly-purchased blanket from Pivnick's Dry Goods Store in Sutton. Only my family has to have this freak tree, whose roots (or boughs?) heave up through the earth in places, and, for most of the area, shade it so thoroughly that no grass grows. The end result is that our graves resemble, instead of the neatly counterpaned plots of their neighbour's, a child's first attempt at gardening. What grass comes up is stubbly and meagre; the few flowers and shrubs we have planted soon wither with discouragement.

Then, too, Granny had decided, before she died, against individual tombstones, generously inviting her children to inscribe their names on the blank portions of her stone. The effect is rather like a census record, or a village roll call. Granny also decided that a small marker, with the incumbent's Christian name on it, should be sunk at the head of each grave . . . out of consideration to the grave-tender, I imagine. I do not suppose she fully anticipated the effect of this large, barish area, with the small stones inscribed with the diminutive names of her children: "Dot," "Daisy," "Jim," "Dick," etc. One's first impression is that this is a burying place for the family pets. "Dot" . . . the family beagle, perhaps? "Daisy" . . . a loved kitten? "Jim" and "Dick" . . . a team of workhorses, maybe? Since Uncle Stephen's name was rarely shortened, his marker does have some dignity; yet, in that informal congregation, one would not have easily guessed that this is the grave of a human. "Stephen" might, after all be the name of some distinguished breed of dog . . . say, a dachshund, or a wolfhound.

Still, at least his place *was* ready for him in the churchyard, and it really was his own fault if his funeral turned out to be a bit of a hodge-podge, and not what the public might have looked forward to when they buried their most famous man of letters.

To begin with, as I remarked earlier, he timed his death badly. It is true he waited till the day after Uncle Martyn Sibbald had died to make his exit; but he should have waited another week. As it was, either the Sibbalds decided to hold Uncle Martyn over an extra day, or perhaps Uncle Stephen was cheated of one of his allotted three days of grace before he was hurried before his Maker. At any rate, the two old friends (they had been close, even though Uncle Martyn was quite a few years old than Uncle Stephen) were buried on the same day. It was, as one reporter remarked, a Double Feature; and as one who sat through both – well, shows – I can vouch that it was one of the least enjoyable I have ever attended.

The theatre – pardon me, the church . . . was cold, to begin with, and the seats – pews, that is – were unpadded and as chilly as slabs of ice. By the time we had sat through the main attraction (Uncle Martyn's service) we were shaking from the cold, and almost longing for the outdoors, where at least we would be able to move about, however decorously, and stamp our feet.

We who had driven from Belleville, and, I imagine, others in our family, had not known till we got to the church that Uncle Martyn had died, absorbed in our own sorrow as we had been. And I think it quite possible that some of the Suttonians and friends of the Sibbald family may not have known of Uncle Stephen's death, nor that he was to be buried on the same day.

Uncle George grasped the fact as soon as he was seated, and realized that the service which the minister was leading us through was not for his brother, but for Uncle Martyn.

"By golly, Mary, it's a Double Feature," he whispered quite loudly enough to be heard to the back of the church.

At any rate, although a few people left directly after Uncle Martyn's graveside service was over, most of them, though they gazed wistfully at their cars, did the polite thing, and filed back into the church for Uncle Stephen's rites. So the physical discomfort, not to overlook the odd feeling of "I have been here before . . . and recently," as the minister started to intone the service all over again, made the Double Feature Funeral memorable, even to those to whom funerals were commonplace, and Uncle Stephen's fame a matter of indifference.

Not only did we repeat the words of the funeral service. We even sang some of the same hymns twice, Uncle Martyn and Uncle Stephen apparently having shared the same tastes in ecclesiastical music.

Altogether, one had the sensation, during my uncle's service, that one should leave and make room for the second audience, which, one expected, was waiting in a patient queue outside. As a matter of fact, as we trooped out of the church after Uncle Martyn's coffin, we heard, from the other side of the high cedar hedge, the hearty voice of the Sutton police who had been assigned to keep back the crowds. (No one had thought to inform the Sutton police that Uncle Stephen's funeral was to be private, and the general public definitely excluded.) The officer's voice cut through the clergyman's mournful words, as Uncle Martyn sank slowly into his grave. "Plenty of room inside!" came the reassuring words, over the hedge. "Plenty of room! Just move along, please! Plenty more room! Plenty more room!" It was a moment or two before we realized that he was assuring late arrivals of parking space, not accommodation in a grave.

Not content with mucking up the church part of the program, Uncle Stephen further marred the normally smooth operation of a Leacock funeral by choosing a big show-off casket instead of the fifty-buck box. His was a monstrous affair of mahogany or oak — I cannot remember which — but it was ostentatiously grained and burled, with big, horehound taffy sworls and swirls, all varnished or veneered over till the whole contraption shone as if it had just come from the confectioner's tray. It had rich handles on it, too (each of them must have cost about $25, from what I know of funerary hardware).

Seeing this huge, solid container, those pallbearers who came from within the family immediately recognized that, used as they were to a nice balancing of the flimsy fifty-buck box, they must put forth all their strength if they were not to buckle beneath the weight of Uncle Stephen and his massive case. So they heaved mightily — and the thing nearly flew out of their hands. The Leacock pallbearers – or, at any rate, the more determined, or huskier of them – must have chosen the aft end of the box (or the head of the corpse, have it as you will), for this end jerked up into the air, and Uncle Stephen nearly stubbed his toes against the frozen earth of the churchyard. What the pallbearers had not known, apparently, was that my uncle had had himself cremated, and that heavy though the Big City box might be, there was only a few grams of ashes inside it, so that the total weight was considerably lighter than that of a fifty-buck box plus cadaver.

I remember very little else of my uncle's graveside service except that it was, if you will pardon the expression, perishingly cold, with a truly biting wind coming in off the lake. We rarely cry at funerals, and we had had, after all, several days to accustom ourselves to the idea that my uncle might die; so it was as likely that our unusually copious floods of tears may have been evoked by the heartless wind as by sorrow. We were, after all, schooled to meet the gradual passing from our scene of these wonderful uncles and aunts who had made of our childhood such a miraculous thing; nor did we, true Britishers-by-descent, and descendants of our staunch Granny, hold with giving way to emotion.

However, there was one further incident which took place at the actual burial, and made us all feel much better. The grave came very close beneath a far-stretched limb of the Upside-Down Tree, which had been propped up with a slab of wood. The plank had been pulled out before the grave was dug, and lay in readiness for the grave-digger to replace it after the funeral. Uncle George, seeing the rough beam lying close to the undertaker's bright green phony grass, and the gleaming metal framework of the little elevator contraption by which the box would be let down (sinking, sinking, sinking, ever so much more smoothly and gracefully than my uncle ever moved in life), realized at once what it was for.

"By God," he exclaimed in delight, hard on the minister's solemn "Amen!," "even when he's dead, they have to put a post on him to keep him down." Then we all laughed, and for a moment it seemed that it was a normal Leacock funeral, and that Uncle Stephen was enjoying it with us.

Most of the family stopped at Meadowlea, Uncle George's place at Aurora, for something to warm us up before we proceeded on to our homes in Toronto or Belleville. I recall Uncle George being quieter, and testier, than he ordinarily was. We could usually count on him to get us over these rough spots in our family history. But it must have been a very, very hard thing for Uncle George to accustom himself to Stephen's absence. Even though Uncle Stephen was one of the "big boys," these two were always very close – in the nimbleness of their minds, in the originality and apparently inexhaustible wealth of their wit.

There was an immediate and very painful sequel to Uncle Stephen's funeral ahead for us at Belleville.

Uncle Charlie, who had been suffering from one of the repeated fits of mental depression which had made a tragedy of his life, and had condemned this brilliant engineer to a life of almost complete idleness, came out of hospital for the funeral. After the ceremony he drove to Belleville with us, to visit for a while.

If Uncle Stephen's death had been hard on Uncle George, at least he was in good health, and could bring the fortitude he had learned earlier to help him combat his sorrow. But to poor Uncle Charlie, the most sensitive one of all the brothers, and, although possessed of a good sense of humour, of a generally more serious turn of mind than the others, the death of his adored brother was agonizing.

At Belleville, as we sat about the fire after the long trip, we tried to be cheerful, for my mother's sake, and Uncle Charlie joked and did his best to rise above his grief. Then he began to tell a story he had heard Uncle Stephen tell.

There was a very strong physical resemblance between these two brothers, and between their voices as well; and Uncle Charlie, like them all, had the gift of mimicry. As Uncle Charlie told the story he, quite literally, stepped into the part of Uncle Stephen completely. Strangely, uncomfortably, he *became* Uncle Stephen.

As I listened to him that day I learned that what the phrase "spine-prickling" means. To hear Uncle Stephen's voice coming from my tortured Uncle Charlie, to see the same blue-grey eyes looking out from a face that seemed to have changed subtly, into that of my dead uncle's . . . it was, literally, as if the newly-dead walked again.

To make it even more harrowing, this was not the merry, happy uncle we had known. The words that broke forth from that mouth were terrible words, for, as if driven by the goad of memory, Uncle Charlie vented forth thoughts he had never allowed himself to utter before. Frightful feelings were expressed . . . uncertainties, doubts . . . hatred, bitterness . . . fear, shaking, white fear . . . thoughts and words which, indeed, Uncle Stephen may never, in reality, have allowed past his lips, but which Uncle Charlie, with his inside track to his brother's mind, divined as clearly as if they had been spoken. And they issued from Uncle Charlie's lips in Uncle Stephen's voice, there could be no mistaking it. Not a note, not a shade that was not exactly true.

It was that evening, in my father's house, that Uncle Charlie said of Uncle Stephen, "He was a man, I tell you, of terrible despairs . . . a man beset with doubts."

Yet of all these thoughts which Uncle Charlie relayed, of all the terrible translations from Uncle Stephen's mind, no experience was more awful than to hear that golden, honeycomb voice, and know that it was forever stilled.

There was another, lighter-hearted sequel to the funeral at the lake. It occurred several years after Uncle Stephen's death, when I was living, with my three children, in an old log cabin on the Eildon Hall property, a short distance from the church.

I had been very pleased with myself that morning, as I led my small flock of Leacock descendants (plus Tuffy, the steel-wool terrier) up the dusty lane that ran from the Shack to Sibbald's Church. While I, like my dead uncle, did not hold with graves and with pre-occupation with the left-overs of our mortal life (the dust, the ashes, the bones, the formaldehyde-soaked and insignificant carcass from which crate the person himself has escaped), still, flowers became the little country churchyard, and it made a nice walk for the children and myself. Although, it is true, if the flowers were for anyone, they were for Aunt Dot and Granny.

Most recently deceased and greatly loved by all of us, Aunt Dot had been very much an Establishment type; yet she held within her uncritical heart so much love for all of us, with our strange foibles and excesses and eccentricities, that I am amazed that organ did not burst her small frame. She would, I knew, have been gratified by any evidence that we still retained some respect for convention. Nor can we be certain, I had reflected, that life ends with the stop of the heart, the final expiration of breath. If ghosts can haunt, what more logical place for the departed Leacocks than at Sibbald's Church? As my uncle wrote, in *The Boy I Left Behind Me*, "... the most real of our standing treats and holidays came to us on contract with Lake Simcoe. This grew out of our going every Sunday in summer to the lake shore church four miles away." And he goes on, in the following pages, to describe how they were allowed to swim there, and how they had, as boys, watched the present beautiful grey-stone church being built.

Should Aunt Dot's small ghost return, on a Summer evening, I could imagine its gratification to find our flowers on her grave. And, as ghosts can divine more than humans, and Leacock ghosts, being Irish, have presumably the gift of unusual intuitions, it would likely say, "Isn't that just like Betty? Imagine those twins and the baby walking all the way up from the Shack! And the flowers ... they must be from Betty's garden!"

And so they were; nor had it been without a selfish pang or two that I had plucked the few straggly blooms that had finally sprouted in the plot I had made beside the Shack. If these spindly flowers were the sorriest excuse for the glory promised on the "Old Fashioned Garden" packet, yet they represented an enormous expenditure of man (or woman) hours of back-breaking toil. I had had only a broken-bladed shovel and a Woolworth trowel with which to hack through the hummocky, weed-rooted field grass to lay bare a plot of soil about four by six feet. I had braved, too, garter snakes and bees to bring these buds to birth. Later, squirrels and birds, avid for daintier fodder than the horses' oats and the seeds of field-flowers, had dug up the seed, and the garden had had to be replanted. Water from the rain-barrel, zealously harvested for dishes and for face-washings, had had to be sacrificed to nourish the surviving seeds. The small bouquets which Stephen and Michael bore to the grave represented almost our total floral harvest, and it would be a week or two before we could expect even this stingy showing again. So I was certain that Aunt Dot and Granny, whose grave we also intended to honour, would be touched by our gesture; and hoped that, as our small company set out on its pious pilgrimage, their shades observed us.

It was fairly early in the morning, and the twins' cotton shorts and jerseys and Hughie's seersucker overalls were still clean, as were their faces. We all wore shoes for the occasion, a detail which should indicate its importance. It was, to paraphrase my uncle, a question of caste, not thistles this time. There were no thistles on the dusty, well-trod lane; and to the soles of our feet, toughened up now by nearly two months of going barefoot, and accustomed to trafficking over the sharp stones of the beach, the occasional worn stone or pocket of gravel were luxurious as broadloom. We did not need shoes. In fact, they were a hardship.

Still, we donned shoes for the morning service at the church each Sunday. Admittedly, we carried them in our hands across the orchard, and up the drive from the Hall, putting them on just before we went through the gate and into the churchyard, so that we might make a decent appearance among the other church-goers. (The latter might have blinked with surprise, I sometimes reflected, had they met, five minutes earlier, a young woman dressed in a hand-embroidered white pique dress and picture hat, with prayer book in gloved hand – and with her feet bare. The children, too, were decently got up in clean shorts and blazers – and they, too, carried their sandals and socks in their hands.)

So this morning, equally reverentially, I had put on espadrilles and the boys wore their sandals. Michael, the more serious of the twins, and one who greatly loved ceremony, wore an expression which on the face of an older person would have been described as pompous. Stephen, his older twin (by 25 minutes), had a set view which a stranger might interpret as sorrow; I, who had had a hard time to persuade him to spare an hour from his loved horses, recognized it as grim endurance. The baby simply beamed; he was happy at this excursion into the great world at the end of the lane, nor did he query its purpose. (Our weekdays were spent, generally, at the beach, with stop-offs at the Hall being our only contact outside the Shack.) He held tightly to my hand . . . not only as a safe tether (he was by nature timid) but as support when the going was particularly rough. Tuffy, grinning from ear to ear (he had to; his upper jaw had been broken by a kick from a horse whose heels he had yapped at once too often the summer before) brought up the rear. Not that I had planned his inclusion in our company; realizing that he might cash in on the opportunity afforded by the tombstones, I had locked him inside the Shack. However he had jumped through the window-screen and had followed us.

Although our pilgrimage was primarily in honour of Aunt Dot and Granny, I intended to allow the others, Uncle Stephen among them, the odd blossom. In fact, remembering that only last Sunday I had had to fob off the accustomed politely restrained inquiries about Stephen Leacock's bare, unmarked grave, I thought, as we proceeded up the lane, "Well, I hope this will make the tourists happy." It did not occur to me that one of our family might mark the great man's mould with an offering more personal than I had planned.

Still, it happened.

"HUGHIE, NOT ON UNCLE STEPHEN!"

Stephen's small, shocked voice cut across my dreamy mood, as I bent over Aunt Dot's grave, arranging the flowers I had brought.

I looked up just in time to see the amber arc, sparkling in the sunlight and blessing, with its modest rainbow, the dried grass beneath which lay Uncle Stephen. A small finger of flesh protruded from the fly of the baby's overall. At Stevie's voice the arc wavered, spurted wildly, then resumed its even outline. Its progenitor had obviously heard his brother, but his expression remained rapt. Hugh had always had excellent powers of concentration.

I cannot say that I was shocked. After all, at the Shack we lived more outdoors than in; even when, in the early morning, we exercised the formality of tripping out to the weatherbeaten closet behind the Shack, we were still as much outdoors as in; the roof had gone years before; the door, which faced away from the house and across the fields, was also missing; and so were quite a few boards from the walls. But most of the time, an obliging rock or bush or tree was more practical than formal plumbing, particularly as my offspring were all male. So, to Hughie, what was the difference between a stand of goldenrod, or a wild rosebush, or this handy stone he had found on its patch of grass?

Still, with all the talk of the Leacock family's indifference to the state of the great man's grave, I was glad that there were no onlookers to a deed which might be regarded as wilful irreverence. Through my mind flashed possible headlines in the Sutton newspaper: "VANDALS DESECRATE GRAVE OF FAMOUS NATIVE SON," for instance.

A more cheerful speculation followed upon this thought. Might not Hugh's action be taken as a practical reply to one lady tourist whom I had overheard, a few days before, remark in disgust as she looked at the coarse, burned grass of the unmarked plot: "They might at least keep it watered."

Hugh, at least, had thought to water Uncle Stephen's grave.

Other Canadian Lives you'll enjoy reading

Canadian Lives is a paperback reprint series which presents the best in Canadian biography chosen from the lists of Canada's many publishing houses. Here is a selection of titles in the series. Watch for more Canadian Lives every season, from Goodread Biographies. Ask for them at your local bookstore.

Something Hidden: A Biography of Wilder Penfield
Jefferson Lewis

The life story of a world-famous Canadian surgeon and scientist — written by his journalist grandson who has portrayed both the public and the private sides of Penfield's extraordinary life of achievement.

"One of the most valuable and fascinating biographies I have read in many years." — Hugh MacLennan

Canadian Lives 1   0-88780-101-3

Within the Barbed Wire Fence
Takeo Nakano

The moving story of a young Japanese man, torn from his family in 1942 and sent with hundreds of others to a labour camp in the B.C. interior.

"A poet's story of a man trapped by history and events far beyond his control." — *Canadian Press*

Canadian Lives 2   0-88780-102-1

The Patricks: Hockey's Royal Family
Eric Whitehead

A first-rate chronicle of the four-generation family of lively Irish-Canadians who have played a key role in the history of hockey for more than 70 years.

"A damn good story." — Jack Dulmage, *The Windsor Star*

Canadian Lives 3   0-88780-103-X

Hugh MacLennan: A Writer's Life
Elspeth Cameron

The prize-winning bestseller that chronicles the life of one of Canada's most successful novelists.

"This impressive biography does justice to the man and his work." — Margaret Laurence

Canadian Lives 4   0-88780-104-8

Canadian Nurse in China
Jean Ewen

The story of a remarkable young adventurer who went to war-torn China in the 1930s, met all the heroes of the Chinese Revolution, and survived the terrors and dangers she encountered with her ironic sense of humour intact.

"A remarkably candid book by a no-nonsense nurse."
— Pierre Berton

Canadian Lives 5   0-88780-105-6

An Arctic Man
Ernie Lyall

Sixty-five years in Canada's North — the story of a man who chose the Inuit way of life.

"The main reason I decided to do a book about my life in the north is that I finally got fed up with all the baloney in so many books written about the north." — Ernie Lyall, in the preface.

Canadian Lives 6   0-88780-106-4

Boys, Bombs and Brussels Sprouts
J. Douglas Harvey

One man's irreverent, racy, sometimes heart-breaking, account of flying for Canada with Bomber Command in the Second World War.

"Tells more about what it was like 'over there' than all of the military histories ever written." — *Canadian Press*

Canadian Lives 7   0-88780-107-2

Canada's most famous humourist and the whole Leacock clan.

Tommy Douglas by Doris French Shackleton
The story of one of the most admired — and most successful — politicians of the century.

Troublemaker! by James Gray
Western Canada's best-loved historian chronicles the golden age of the prairies from 1936 to 1955.

Walter Gordon: A Political Memoir
A gentle, passionate patriot's story of his experiences inside official Ottawa in the St. Laurent-Pearson era.

Wheel of Things: Lucy Maud Montgomery by Mollie Gillen
An intimate look at the writer who created Canadian fiction's most memorable young character, Anne of Green Gables.

When I Was Young by Raymond Massey
One of Canada's best-known actors recounts his youth as a Massey, the most "establishment" of Canadian families.

Within the Barbed Wire Fence by Takeo Nakarto
The moving story of a young Japanese man, torn from his family in 1942 and sent to a labour camp in the B.C. interior.

Printed in Canada